D0045805

Policies and People

POLICIES AND PEOPLE

The First Hundred Years of The Bankers Life

by Joseph Frazier Wall

Prentice-Hall, Inc., Englewood Cliffs, New Jersey

Book Design by Joan Ann Jacobus
Art Director: Hal Siegel

Policies and People: The First Hundred Years of The Bankers Life, by
Joseph Frazier Wall
Copyright © 1979 by The Bankers Life Company

Printed in the United States of America
Prentice-Hall International, Inc., London / Prentice-Hall of Australia, Pty. Ltd., Syd-
ney / Prentice-Hall of Canada, Ltd., Toronto / Prentice-Hall of India Private Ltd.,
New Delhi / Prentice-Hall of Japan, Inc., Tokyo / Prentice-Hall of Southeast Asia
Pte. Ltd., Singapore / Whitehall Books Limited, Wellington, New Zealand
10 9 8 7 6 5 4 3 2 1

Library of Congress Cataloging in Publication Data
Wall, Joseph Frazier.
  Policies and people.
  Includes index.
  1. Bankers Life Company—History. I. Title.
HG8963.B362W34   368.3'62   79-11636
ISBN 0-13-684019-1

To the thousands of men and women who have served Bankers Life over the past one hundred years, with a special personal tribute to the memory of Bert N. Mills, a true gentleman, who during his life exemplified the high ideals and standards of the company.

Contents

Policies and People

Prologue/
Yesterday, Des Moines, Iowa

1879

*It had been fourteen years since the immaculately dressed Robert E.
Lee, looking in defeat like an imperturbable Roman conqueror, had
handed over his sword with formal dignity to the rumpled, unkempt
Ulysses S. Grant, looking in victory like a weary, unshaven, back-
woods loser, and the Great American War of Rebellion had at last
ended at a country courthouse called Appomattox in far distant
Virginia. Now those Iowa veterans of the battles of Wilson Creek,
Vicksburg, Shiloh, and Atlanta, who in May 1865 had traveled down
Pennsylvania Avenue to the White House, as one newspaper reporter
commented, "like the lords of the world," were fast approaching
middle age. They had returned to Iowa in 1865 and had settled back
down on their farms or in their small villages, or perhaps driven by
ambition, they had migrated to the state's rapidly growing capital
city, located at the juncture of the Raccoon and Des Moines rivers.*

Fourteen years is a long time in the life of a man, living on the
edge of the frontier and whose adulthood has been severed from his
youth by a great national war. Fourteen years is a time long enough to
see the frontier of his childhood disappear over the western horizon,
retreating only slightly ahead of the rapidly advancing railroads.
Fourteen years is a time sufficient in which to build a city where once
only the empty barracks of an abandoned fort had stood. But on
history's long yardstick, fourteen years occupies a space so infini-
tesimally small as to make the many changes that had occurred in
this nation, this state, and this town since 1865 appear like the
instantaneous flash of a bolt of lightning.

In 1865 the veterans who had come back to Des Moines had found it to be a smaller town than that which they had left, but with their return, they had quickly remedied that. By 1879 the capital city had increased its population sevenfold, and the city boosters were already claiming that Des Moines had now surpassed the old established river towns of Dubuque, Davenport, and Burlington to become Iowa's largest city, a boast that the 1880 census would substantiate by recording Des Moines' population at 22,408.

Although Des Moines had been awarded the state capital by the new state constitution of Iowa in 1857, it was not until a year after the Civil War had ended that the first railroad, the Des Moines Valley Railroad, reached Iowa's remote state capital. The following year, the Chicago, Rock Island, and Pacific Railroad entered Des Moines, and the state capital had at last a direct connection with Chicago and the East Coast. Its rapid growth was now assured.

A visitor coming to Des Moines in the spring of 1879 would have found Iowa's largest town busily making itself into a city. Covering an area of twelve square miles, the town was divided by the river that had given it its name. There was an intense rivalry between the people on the east and those on the west bank of the river. East Des Moines, because it possessed a superb site, a high hill commanding a view of the entire city, had won the bitter contest for the location of the new state capitol building, but the west-siders were more than compensated for that loss by claiming for themselves the railroad yards and depots, the major share of the business offices, hotels, and shops as well as the finest residential areas of the town. From the Rock Island station, the new arrival in Des Moines could look to the east across the river and see the imposingly imperial-Roman-styled capitol building with its four corner domes completed and its great central dome still under construction. "Absolutely fireproof," a local resident might tell the visitor. "The state will never have to pay out anything in the way of fire insurance for that building."

If the visitor turned around and looked to the west, he would see a second imposing edifice which crowned yet another hill that overlooked the juncture of the two rivers. This spectacular diadem was Terrace Hill, the finest Victorian mansion between Chicago and San Francisco, built ten years before by B. F. Allen at the unbelievable cost of a quarter of a million dollars. Allen, who had once been president of three banks in town, no longer lived in the great villa he had built. He had lost everything in the depression of '73, and had been forced to sell Terrace Hill at a fraction of its cost to Frederick Hubbell, who was now reputed to be Iowa's wealthiest citizen.

Both of these hilltop structures, which any visitor to Des Moines would have immediately spotted, were fitting symbols for this new prairie capital. Here encased in stone and brick, adorned with Roman domes and Italianate towers, were housed the political and financial powers of the state. And between the two prestigious hills lay the town, with the oldest wholesale and retail stores, banks, and small manufacturing plants located on the west side of the river, along Second Street for seven blocks between Elm Street on the south edge of the town and Walnut on the northern limit.

The new arrival in Des Moines, walking up Second Street, would probably turn west when he reached Walnut to inspect the more recent business houses that had been built on this northern limit of the business district within the past ten years. At the corner of Second and Walnut his nostrils would be pleasantly assaulted with the spicy sweet smell of cinnamon, or the heavy rich fragrance of fresh-roasted coffee beans. If the aromas of the Tone Brothers Spice Mills whetted his appetite, he could continue up Walnut for a lunch at the Ice Cream and Oyster Parlor at 609 Walnut Street, but if the long night of sitting up in a Rock Island passenger coach had wearied him, he might check in at the new Kirkwood Hotel, which was actually the old Savery House refurbished and renamed. Before going to his room for a short nap, the visitor might pick up a copy of the *Iowa Daily Register*, Des Moines' leading daily newspaper, edited and published by the Clarkson brothers, whose personal and editorial loyalty to Senator William Allison assured them and their paper political prominence within this most Republican of all states.

Glancing through the paper, the visitor might note with interest that the Chicago, Northwestern had just purchased the bankrupt Des Moines and Minnesota Railroad and was now promising that within a year it would provide passenger and freight service to Minneapolis. If the visitor to Des Moines was a farmer or a farm implement dealer, he might be even more interested in reading the announcement that the Iowa State Fair would be held this year for the first time in Iowa's capital city. There would be four glorious days in which to exhibit the state's rich agricultural produce in a new fair building constructed so as "to last for ages, and not the sort to fall to pieces by its own weight."

As must have been apparent to even the most casual observer, Des Moines in 1879 was clearly a city on the make. It was, to be sure, no Chicago or St. Louis, and probably never would be. But now that the depressed decade of the 1870s was coming to an end, there were certainly opportunities here for new people with new ideas. And so by train, by wagon, even by foot, they came—the young and the old, men of means and men of dreams, and the fortunate few who possessed both.

Among the hundreds of those arriving in Des Moines in the spring of 1879 was a middle-aged banker, Edward A. Temple. Unlike most of the others, however, Temple had not come to the capital city to seek wealth or fame. He had already gained enough money and prestige in his small hometown of Chariton, Iowa, to satisfy his simple, ascetic tastes. Nor had he come for adventure; he had known enough of that to last a lifetime when fifteen years earlier he had fought Indians on the Dakota plains and had prospected for gold in the Salmon River region of Idaho. Temple had come to Des Moines because he was possessed of an idea. One of the most prominent citizens of Des Moines, Judge Phineas M. Casady, had expressed considerable interest in that idea, and so Temple had come to the city to explain it in greater detail. His was a rather modest proposal. He wanted to establish an association that could provide inexpensive and dependable life insurance protection for bankers and their employees. That was all he had in mind. As compared to the great railroad systems that were then being constructed across the nation or the giant trusts in steel, oil, and meat-packing that were being organized in these years, this was hardly a business proposal that would shake Wall Street or capture the attention of the business tycoons of Chicago. It would not even rate a paragraph in the local *Iowa Daily Register*. But Edward Temple firmly believed that his proposal would prove to be of some benefit to his banker colleagues. After hearing him out and seeing the letters of support he had received from several other bankers in the state, P. M. Casady and his young banker son, Simon, thought so too. And they were quite right. Mr. Temple's proposal was to prove of considerable benefit to the banking profession—and to the people of the city and the state and the nation as well.

The distinguished historian Johnson Brigham, who for many years served as state librarian of Iowa, wrote a history of Des Moines and Polk County which was published in 1911. In that history, Brigham gave a chronicle of significant events for each year from 1843 up to 1909. For the year 1879, he gave as the most important event: "The Year of Minister Kasson's Return from Vienna. ... The return of

Minister [John] Kasson from Vienna, on a brief vacation, was the occasion of a demonstration on the evening of June 25. A torchlight procession passed through the principal streets into the court house where Chairman Runnells delivered an eloquent address of welcome, to which Mr. Kasson fittingly responsed." Clearly, historian Brigham was hard pressed to come up with a significant event for the year 1879. Had he been truly gifted with the omniscience of the history Muse, Clio, Brigham might have substituted June 24 for June 25 and noted that on that day the Bankers Life Association had filed its Articles of Incorporation with the Secretary of State of Iowa. But there had been no torchlight procession to the office of the Secretary of State on that day, no brass bands to herald the birth of what even one of its own midwives, Simon Casady, had called "the quiet, insignificant child" of Edward Temple's conception. A century of time, however, can provide even the dullest of historians with some of Clio's wonderful hindsight. It is not difficult for us now to see that for Des Moines the most significant event of 1879 was the visit of Edward Temple to the Casadys, an occasion before which even the return of Minister Kasson for a brief vacation pales into insignificance.

1/Mr. Temple's Association
1879-1911

Edward A. Temple is representative of that large class of small-town businessmen of honesty and integrity in the post-Civil War era whom historians tend to ignore in their pursuit of the robber barons and industrial tycoons of the Gilded Age. It has been the Drews, the Goulds, and the Fisks, the Rockefellers, the Carnegies, and the McCormicks who have grabbed the pages of the history books. As a consequence, we tend to forget the thousands and thousands of Temples and Casadys, Kurtzes, Frankels, and Younker brothers, whose daily activities in operating the small-town banks or in selling hardware items, men's pants, and dry goods touched most directly on the day-by-day economic life of most Americans. These small-town businessmen, mostly bred and schooled in strict Judeo-Christian ethics and fully expecting to have to live out their lives under the constantly vigilant scrutiny of their hometown neighbors, could never imagine themselves daring or even wanting to echo William Vanderbilt's curse, "The public be damned." They were as genuinely shocked at the time of the attempted gold market cornering in 1869 by James Fisk's triumphant cry, "Nothing is lost save honor," as later liberal historians have been. To the village merchant and banker, honor was not only a way of life but also an essential policy for staying in business. A man's word given orally and in private had to be as good as any formal legal document, for in a small town the private spoken word was quickly a matter of open public record.

Edward Temple's ethical credentials were well established throughout the state long before he called upon the Casadys in 1879. Born in Lebanon, Illinois, in 1831, Edward Temple was brought to

Burlington, Iowa, by his parents in 1837, only five years after the Black Hawk War of 1832 had opened the eastern part of Iowa to white settlement. His father, George Temple, very quickly distinguished himself in Iowa politics by being elected to Iowa's first territorial legislative assembly in 1838. He subsequently became Speaker of the House in the General Assembly after Iowa became a state in 1846.

Young Edward ended his formal education at the age of fifteen to accept a clerkship in the Burlington post office. Within a year he had become deputy postmaster. In 1849 he left Burlington to become a partner in the firm of Henn, Williams and Company of Fairfield, a company that dealt in land sales and veterans' land warrant claims. Two years later, the twenty-one-year-old Temple was placed in charge of the company's branch office in Chariton, Iowa, a small town some forty miles south of Des Moines.

In 1857 Edward and his brother, George, formed their own land office company. It was an inauspicious year in which to start a new business. Within months after Temple Brothers had opened its doors for business, the Panic of 1857 forced into bankruptcy their New York correspondent, John Thompson, a banker at No. 2 Wall Street, with whom they had deposited most of their ready cash. The Temple brothers received out of the liquidation proceedings only an 8 percent return of their deposits. Refusing to follow Thompson's easy way out through bankruptcy, Edward and George Temple sold their own properties for whatever price they could get, and over the next four years they struggled to pay back all of their creditors in full plus 10 percent interest.

By 1862 Edward Temple was at last able to see an honorable conclusion to the many creditor claims against him and his brother. The Thompson affair had been a devastating blow to his youthful dreams of quick financial success, but out of that disaster Edward Temple had gained two valuable assets: one, he had learned to be forever after wary of eastern, and particularly of Wall Street, finance; and two, he had firmly established his own reputation for integrity and his credit throughout the state of Iowa. Here was a man whose word was his contract, who paid his creditors in full plus the legal interest. All things considered, it was not a bad dividend that Temple had earned out of the Panic of '57.

But weary of the long struggle to achieve financial solvency in Iowa, Temple and his wife, Elizabeth, decided in 1862 to head west, lured by tales of new gold finds in Idaho which might even surpass the California bonanza of 1849. After a harrowing five-month trip by mule team across the plains in which they were pursued and attacked by Indians, they reached Idaho City in the early fall. Temple found no gold lying within easy reach in the creek beds, so he turned to the one business he knew best. He opened up a land claim office which, with a nice touch of irony, he named "No. 2 Wall Street." Here in a tent for an office, he dealt in real estate, mining claims, and Civil War greenback exchange. His canvas shelter did not attract many customers in December, however, once the bitter cold winds swept down from the Canadian Rockies, so Temple folded up his "No. 2 Wall Street" with even less ceremony than his erstwhile partner, Thompson, had closed up the original "No. 2" office. Temple joined his wife who had gone on to the west coast, and shortly thereafter, he became chief quartermaster in the Army for the troops stationed at Fort Vancouver.

With the conclusion of the Civil War, Temple received a release from the Army, and like most other veterans his thoughts turned toward home. In July 1866 he was back in Chariton, where he quickly found employment as resident manager of the Chariton branch of the F. W. Brooks banking firm, which in 1870 became the First National Bank of Chariton with Temple as cashier. Here in this small county seat of Lucas County, he and his wife built their home and with the far western adventures behind them, prepared to spend the rest of their lives.

The small-town banker, like the doctor, lawyer, and preacher, frequently serves as counselor to people in trouble and needing advice. Temple, whose early reputation for integrity and sound financial management had been even further enhanced by his bank's successful weathering of the great 1873 depression, was often consulted by the farmers and townspeople of Chariton on financial matters that were only tangentially related to the banking business.

Many of the questions most frequently asked of Temple by young men with families to support were related to life insurance: "Is it advisable to have some life insurance?" "Is it safe to invest my hard-earned dollars in some distant company I know nothing about?" "Is it moral to gamble with fate on how long I shall live?" These were the questions that Temple was asked time and again, forcing him to do what research he could into the whole question of life insurance. What he discovered from the little information that was available was not very reassuring.

Although the concept of life insurance is an old one, dating perhaps as far back as the time of the Roman Empire, it had its first rudimentary beginnings in modern history in connection with marine insurance. In the seventeenth century it became a common practice to insure the life of the merchant who was accompanying his goods against death or capture by pirates for the duration of the sea voyage. A little later, fraternal societies, such as the Order of Freemasons, in the eighteenth century began to provide death benefits for their members by levying an assessment upon the surviving members whenever anyone of their society died.

The first true commercial life insurance to be formed unrelated to fraternal organizations was the Society of Assurance for Widows and Orphans, organized in London in 1699, but the first several death claims made against its inadequate funds quickly drove the company out of business. In 1706 the Amicable Society for a Perpetual Assurance was chartered by Queen Anne, and only then can it be said that the modern life insurance business began. The Amicable Society functioned successfully for over 150 years. Its continuing success was due, however, to careful management and close scrutiny of applicants, not to any understanding of how to determine accurate premium rates based upon scientific actuarial tables.

The great mathematical genius and philosopher Blaise Pascal as early as 1684 provided the basic mathematical formula for the doctrine of changes upon which the entire science of life contingencies is based by demonstrating with a pair of dice that given a sufficiently large number of happenings in the past, he could with absolute precision predict the number of happenings that would occur in the future. The British astronomer Edmund Halley quickly applied this idea to mortality rates. However, it was not until fifty years later than any practical application was made of Pascal's and Halley's theories of probabilities. In 1762 the Equitable Society for the Assurance of Life and Survivorship was formed in London, and for the first time premium rates were based upon a mortality table, one that had been prepared by Dr. Richard Price from an enumeration of deaths in the town of Northampton, England, over a forty-six-year period. Price's data were fragmentary and inaccurate, but at least the Equitable Society was grasping for sound principles upon which to establish rates.

The first commercial life insurance companies in the United States, the Presbyterian Ministers' Fund, organized in Philadelphia in 1759, and the Mutual Life Insurance Company of New York, formed eighty years later, were hardly more advanced in actuarial science than were their British counterparts. It was not until Sheppard

Homans designed the American Experience Table in 1859 based upon the mortality experience of the Mutual Life Insurance Company over a fifteen-year period that insurance companies at last had available a scientifically accurate table upon which to base their premiums. Only then could the business of life insurance approach that standard which Homans himself so rhapsodically set for it when he wrote in his article on "Life Insurance" for the study *One Hundred Years of American Commerce*, published in 1896:

> *Life insurance is one of the most beneficent devices of modern civilization. By its means the pecuniary loss and hardship which would result to a family from the death of its natural protector are assumed by a vast number of persons, upon each of whom such loss falls lightly. It is benevolence without ostentation, and charity without humiliation. It is practically a fulfillment of the divine injunction to "bear one another's burdens," and is therefore an evidence of the highest Christian civilization.*

The conservative and conscientious Edward Temple, sitting in his bank office in Chariton, Iowa, in the late 1860s could not wax quite as lyrical as Homans over the Christian values of life insurance, however, when he was asked by his customers if they should buy life insurance. The Civil War had undoubtedly had a great impact upon the general public's interest in life insurance. Prior to the war, life insurance had been mainly a concern of the rich. For the poor, if one was young and healthy, death was something one tried not to think about, and if one was old and sick, one could only hope that one's children would provide for a proper burial. But the war with its mass carnage of the young and the healthy had made death a familiar visitor. Returning veterans with vivid memories of their tent-mates sitting next to them, laughing and joking one minute and the next moment lying dead, were preoccupied as they had never been before with the uncertainty and temporality of life.

Inevitably, interest created a supply, even an oversupply, of new life insurance companies, which in turn, by offering their agents exorbitant commissions to push life insurance sales, further heightened the interest. By 1869 there were some 110 companies in the United States selling life insurance, and many of these companies were providing policies with some very fine print indeed. Most of them provided for no grace period whatsoever. If the premium was not paid every month by the specified date, the policy was canceled and it carried no surrender value whatsoever. Any change of occupation or even long-distance travel could void many policies, and a misstatement of some trivial fact in the application or medical report, discovered years later by the company after many premiums had been paid, could also be a cause for cancellation of the policy. Death may be certain to all mortal beings, but many insurance companies were relying on another certainty occurring first, human error, which would allow them to collect many premiums without having to pay out the death benefits.

Most of the insurance companies, moreover, were located in the East, and with his suspicion of all eastern financial agencies, born of his own bitter experience, Temple was reluctant to advise his friends and associates to hand their hard cash over to New York "speculators" as he had once done. It is true that Iowa now had its own major home-based life insurance company, Equitable Life of Iowa, which had been established in Des Moines in 1867 with Hubbell and Allen money. Temple was convinced, however, that even with a reputable local firm like Equitable, the premium rates were far in excess of what was needed to provide adequate coverage. Too much money had to be kept in reserve to meet death claims, too much was spent on commissions for salesmen, on salaries and office expenses. There must be a better, less expensive way for those honest associates and employees of his and his fellow bankers who wanted assured protection for their families.

Quite by accident, some time in the mid-1870s, Temple heard of a professional assessment plan that provided him with the inspiration he needed for a resolution of the problem that was troubling him. His brother, George, living in Fairfield, had taken into his home a visiting Episcopalian minister, who soon after his arrival became stricken with what was quite apparently a mortal affliction. Shortly before his death, the minister told George's wife, who was nursing him, that he belonged to a ministerial life assessment association. This association was limited to one hundred ministers who had agreed that whenever one of their members died, the other ninety-nine would each pay his beneficiary ten dollars, and at that point one new minister would be invited in to replace the departed brother. The dying minister asked Mrs. Temple, in the event of his death, to write to the association's secretary, who would then mail to his widow a check for $990. Upon the death of the minister, Mrs. Temple carried out his last instructions, and a short while later the Temples heard from the minister's widow that she had promptly received the death payment which had been more than adequate to cover the burial expenses.

Knowing of his brother's interest in life insurance plans, George Temple related this story to Edward. Here was the nucleus around which the Temple plan was to be built. Edward Temple was intrigued by several aspects of this ministerial assessment idea: first, it was limited to a single non-hazardous profession where the expected mortality rate would be low; second, operational expenses were at an absolute minimum, limited mainly to stationery and postage stamps to inform the members of the association that one of their members had died and asking them to pay up; third, no reserve was necessary—it was strictly a pay-as-someone-goes proposition. If a group of ministers could form what was apparently a very successful life assessment association, why could not bankers and their employees, who were engaged in an equally nonhazardous, low-risk occupation, form a similar association?

The one feature of the ministerial plan that troubled Temple was the strict limit on number of members in the association. This, to be sure, was its strength—the careful selection of each new member and the strict limit of obligation for assessment that each member in the association had. But Temple felt this limitation on number of members in the association was also a weakness. If he could design a simple, inexpensive program for bankers and bank employees, he wanted it to be available to more than a small, rigidly fixed number. He wanted an association that could grow with demand, not an elite club into which one could be admitted only by a vacancy created by death.

Once he began to think in terms of an expandable association, however, he had to face up to other problems. Most fraternal societies had failed in their life assessment plans because they were not cognizant of one basic fact of life—the death rate for youths is quite low, but it increases rapidly as any given population group becomes older. A fraternal assessment program would initially attract many young people because its rates were low, but with each passing year unless more and more young could be brought in, the assessment would become higher and higher. The younger members would drop out, the older members could eventually be unable to pay the even higher assessments, and the program would fold.

Temple probably knew nothing of Pascal's and Halley's scientific doctrines of chances. He may have had no real knowledge of

Sheppard Homans' carefully formulated American Experience Table. But he did have enough rudimentary knowledge of mortality rates to devise a plan that incorporated the concept that all payments made by the members should be based upon the age of the member at entry.

Temple also realized that although he wanted no large reserves such as that required of all mutual life insurance companies, some kind of emergency reserve fund would be necessary in case, in any one year, there might be claims in excess of the 10 deaths per 1,000 that he drew from the U.S. Census report as his basic mortality rate figure.

After months of pondering and many discussions with banker friends and with others more knowledgeable than they in the field of insurance, Temple finally developed his assessment plan. Certificates, each with a face value of $2,000, would be made available to bankers and bank employees. Applicants between the ages of twenty-one and thirty-six years were limited to the purchase of three certificates, or $6,000 worth of insurance; applicants between the ages of thirty-five and fifty years might purchase two certificates; and those between fifty-one and fifty-five were limited to only one certificate. No one under the age of twenty-one or over the age of fifty-five was eligible for membership.

If accepted as a member, the applicant made an initial guarantee deposit of one dollar for each year of his age for each certificate he purchased. Thus a new member, aged forty, would pay an initial guarantee deposit fee of $80 if he bought the two certificates to which he was entitled. If he kept his membership in force until the time of his death, the original guarantee deposit would be returned to his beneficiary along with the death payment. If, however, he allowed his membership to lapse, this deposit fee would be placed in a reserve fund, along with all interest that the association had earned in its investment of payments made by the members.

In addition to the guarantee deposit, the new member paid an initiation fee, also based upon his age at entry, of one half of his guarantee deposit. Thus the aforementioned forty-year-old member who purchased two certificates would pay an initiation fee of $40. This initiation fee was not returnable. It went into a so-called contingent fund which was to be used for operating expenses: medical examinations, commissions, office expenses, and supplies.

For the initial sum of $120, the successful forty-year-old applicant had a life insurance coverage of $4,000. Once a member of the association, he was subject to quarterly assessment calls to pay for the actual death losses that occurred within that quarter of the year.

Each member would be assessed a certain percentage of his guarantee deposit which was based upon his age at entry, but in no event would the yearly assessment calls exceed 1 percent of the total amount of insurance in force. Compared to the prevailing rates charged by the regular commercial or mutual life insurance companies, even this maximum amount would be relatively inexpensive. Temple figured, however, that with the careful selection of members into the association that he anticipated, the actual death rate should be considerably lower than the national average of 10 per 1,000 population. The annual assessment calls for our hypothetical forty-year-old, $4,000 certificate holder would be but a fraction of what he would have to pay for the same coverage under ordinary life insurance programs.

In case of some unexpected disaster, however, in which the deaths for any one year should exceed 1 percent of the membership, the excess payments for these claims would be drawn from the reserve fund, which, as noted above, would consist of forfeited guarantee deposits plus the interest earned in all income the association had invested. And the association would be limited in its investments to "registered bonds of the United States government." In Temple's plan of operations, there would be no reckless speculation of the association's funds in Wall Street stock or high-risk commercial ventures.

That in substance was the Temple Plan: as simple in design and as unadorned with any gimcrackery as a Greek Ionic temple. No excessive reserves, no dividends to pay out, no unnecessary expenses. With this plan in hand, Temple consulted with banker friends in Marshalltown, Fairfield, Burlington, Creston, and Albia, and from each he got a strong vote of confidence. In the spring of 1879, upon his arrival in Des Moines, he got the endorsement of the powerful Casady family. On May 1, 1879, the Articles of Incorporation were drawn up:

Article 1. Name. This Association shall be known and designated as "The Bankers Life Association." Article 2. Object. The object of this Association shall be the creation of a fund by making mutual pledges and giving valid obligations of the members to each other for their own insurance from loss by death; the preservation of the fund from mismanagement and loss by the judicious investment of the same in registered bonds of the United States; and the equitable distribution of that fund among the families or designated beneficiaries of deceased members.

The remaining articles provided for the home office to be located in Des Moines, and established a Board of Directors to consist of P. M. Casady, Dr. George Glick of Marshalltown, M. S. Smalley of Galesburg, Illinois, B. F. Elbert of Albia, and Edward Temple. On June 11 the Articles were filed and recorded in the Polk County courthouse and on June 24 with the Secretary of State.

On July 1, 1879, the five directors met in the back room of the Casadys' Des Moines Bank located on the southwest corner of Third and Walnut streets and elected officers: Edward A. Temple, President; P. M. Casady, Vice-President; Simon Casady, Secretary; and Lyman Cook, who was president of the First National Bank of Burlington, Treasurer. The three directors not elected to office were designated as follows: M. S. Smalley, Financial Director; Dr. George Glick, Medical Director; and B. F. Elbert, Judicial Director. The Bankers Life Association was formally in business. The first certificate for $2,000 was not issued until September 2, however. Quite appropriately it went to Temple, with Certificate No. 2 issued to Simon Casady.

At the end of 1879, when the Association was six months old, the annual statement listed $108,000 (or fifty-four certificates) of insurance in force. There was $1,942 in the guarantee fund, $77.28 in the benefit fund (apparently a very small assessment had been called even though no deaths had occurred), $349.23 in the contingent fund for expenses, and nothing in the reserve fund since no certificates had been forfeited and no interest as yet had accumulated.

The earliest certificates issued by the Association, although referred to as $2,000 certificates, bore the notation from the Association's constitution that "each certificate shall entitle the heirs or legal representatives, or designated beneficiary of a deceased member to a sum of money equal to 2 percent, of the aggregate amount of the Guarantee Fund, as may appear by the books of the Association on the first day of the month in which the death of such member may occur, provided that the beneficiary of a deceased member shall not receive over TWO THOUSAND DOLLARS for each Certificate of membership issued to or held by such deceased member."

No death occurred among the members of the Association for nearly three years after the Association began operations. It was not until June 15, 1882, that a check was issued to the beneficiaries of William H. Lloyd, late cashier of the Brighton (Iowa) National Bank. They received a check for $453 for Lloyd's certificate, since at the moment of his death the guarantee fund stood at $22,650. By March of 1884, however, the fund had grown to $100,000, and from that time on all death claims were paid at the full amount of the certificate.

The future success of the Temple Plan of Assessment Life Insurance depended upon several factors. Of major importance was the necessity for continual expansion. Because the assessment was fixed at 1 percent per year as an upper limit, it was absolutely essential to bring in new young members at a constantly increasing rate. Not only would more youths offset the growing mortality rate of the older members of the Association but the increased guarantee deposit funds would inevitably augment the emergency reserve fund which could be drawn upon when the mortality rate exceeded 1 percent in any one year. Perhaps one of the most important decisions the Board of Directors of Bankers Life made over the past century occurred at the very first meeting of the Board on July 1, 1879. At that time a resolution was passed extending membership not only to bankers and their employees, the group for whom Temple had originally designed his plan, but to anyone else that the depository banks might recommend for membership who could meet the strict standards set by the Association. Very quickly, the Association began soliciting new members outside of Iowa. As early as 1883, Bankers Life was doing business in the state of New York and was taking business away from the big New York life insurance companies in their home state, much to Temple's delight. Other states were soon entered: Michigan and Nebraska in 1885, Minnesota and Ohio in 1886, Missouri and Colorado in 1887. By the turn of the century Bankers Life was an association open for membership to the residents of twenty-one states. Explicitly excluded, however, by formal resolution of the Board were all states south of the 36° 30' latitude, the old parallel line that had divided the free territory from the slave territory in the Missouri Compromise. The reason given by the Board for this geographical discrimination was that of health. It was feared that a higher mortality rate in the South due to yellow fever, dysentery, and malaria presented too great a risk to warrant accepting members from places like South Carolina and Texas. But one suspects that for most of the Board the passions engendered by the Civil War had not totally subsided. An old veteran like Temple, even though his army service in Vancouver, Washington, was about as far removed as it could have been from the battlefields of Virginia and Georgia, was still an ardent Union patriot. One cannot imagine him welcoming any damned Rebels into his beloved Association. This suspicion of sectional bias is strenthened by the fact that Missourians, Californians, and Nevadans were acceptable to the Association, even though their states lay in part south of the forbidden line. Missouri, California, and Nevada, it is hardly necessary to add, had all remained loyal states to the Union cause.

If the Association from the beginning of its actual operations was not limited to bank employees, nevertheless banks continued to play a central role in Temple's plan. Certain banks in communities throughout the several states in which the Association did business were designated as depository banks. Not only did these banks serve as credit clearing agencies to pass approval on applicants for membership, but they also served as centers for the deposit of assessment calls and guarantee deposits and initiation fees for new members. The depository banks would collect these moneys and would then send a certified check for funds collected to the home office at the end of each month. In return they got free use of the money during the month in which they collected it. In tellers' windows throughout the Middle and Far West, bank customers could spot the familiar little green card: "Bankers Life Calls May Be Paid Here." For these services the bank received two thirds of the initiation fee of new members. Thus, the small-town bankers, who were frequently asked about insurance by their customers as Temple had been, became The Bankers Life Association's earliest insurance salesmen.

During the early years of the Association before an elaborate agency system had been developed, the designated depository banks did yeoman service for Bankers Life. By 1894 there were 2,376 depository banks throughout the sixteen states in which Bankers Life did business. The cashier of each of the earliest designated depository banks also served as "councillor" for the Association. Proposed policy changes were submitted to the councillors for their recommendations and advice. On at least one occasion, in 1884, it was the councillors' negative response that prevented the Board of Directors from adopting a change in the by-laws that would have allowed the officers to invest funds in state, county, and school district bonds as well as in United States registered bonds, to which they were then limited. As the number of depository banks grew, however, the Board of Councillors became so large that it could no longer effectively serve as an advisory board to the Association, and it seems to have been quietly forgotten. But the individual banks remained important agencies for the Association until well into the twentieth century. And there is in the minutes of the Board but a single entry to indicate that on one occasion only was a designated depository bank removed from the list for failure to perform its services in a satisfactory manner.

Throughout the 1880s and 1890s the Association showed a steady if not spectacular growth in membership. By 1882 it had over $2 million worth of insurance in force, and by the end of that decade, in 1889, that figure had been multiplied eleven fold.

Growth was certainly essential to the Association, but at the same time growth also presented a threat to what had to be another major concern of the Association if it was to survive. Major emphasis had to be given to the careful selectivity of membership if the Association was to keep its mortality rates safely below the 1 percent figure that Temple had set. In other words, quality of membership was as crucial as was quantity, and by quality the Association's officers meant something in addition to the mere passing of a medical examination. For Temple and his fellow officers quite obviously the most desirable habitat for the human species lay along the 42° parallel of the North American continent. The farther one strayed from that temperate line, the greater the danger to life and limb, lungs and bowels. As has been noted, all of the United States below 36° 30′ was forbidden territory (except for Missouri, California, and Nevada). All of Canada, except for the southernmost portion of Ontario province, was also off limits. The early minutes show a great preoccupation of the Board with the question of residency: Levi Johnson of Oskaloosa, Iowa, lost his certificate in 1885 because he was foolish enough to leave that earthly paradise to take a trip to Africa; and Verner Lyman of Kearney, Nebraska, had to surrender his certificate in 1895 because he wanted to reside in China. It was not until the United States began to emerge on the world scene as a great power that Bankers Life began to recognize the outside world. In 1897 the Board rather reluctantly permitted a certificate holder to live in Hawaii for one year only, and later that year, it gave its permission for a member to take up residency in Palermo, Sicily, which was indeed a generous, if not foolhardy, concession. And by 1903 permission was granted to Levi Ostrander of Olympia, Washington, "to visit and reside in Japan and China as requested in his letter dated December 25, 1903." By 1905, when a certificate holder was allowed to live in Nome, Alaska, geographical restrictions except for the Deep South were largely forgotten.

Occupational hazards were also a constant worry for the officers. Resolution No. 85½ of the Board (1885) rejected all applicants who were police officers on the ground that this was "too hazardous an occupation," and in 1901 the Board denied a request of a certificate holder to enter the military service and keep his membership in the Association, even though the United States was officially at peace. Patriotism or policy—it was a hard choice.

The greatest concern for quality, however, was directed toward the personal habits of the individual members. On December 30, 1885, the Board passed a resolution stating that hereafter there would be no payment of death benefit for a deceased member "if death occurred from *willful* self-destruction, or if a member is habitually intemperate in the use of intoxicating liquors, chloral, cocaine or opium." And the Association's definition of intemperate did not far exceed that set by the WCTU. Depository bank officials as well as local physicians who did physical examinations for Bankers Life were expected to report not only on the personal habits of applicants for membership but also on those who were already members but whose conduct had become less than desirable. And report they did. Poor Henry L. Briggs was forced to surrender his three certificates in 1889 because it was reported that "he has become addicted to intemperate habits."

Undoubtedly such policies in respect to residency, occupation, and personal habits had an adverse effect upon growth, but at the same time they had a quite beneficial impact upon the mortality rates of the members. Through war, depression, epidemic, and flood in the late nineteenth century, Bankers Life kept its mortality rate among its members well below the 1 percent of the national average. During the entire thirty-two years of The Bankers Life Association's existence, not once did the officers have to make a withdrawal from the emergency reserve fund because the mortality rate had exceeded the 1 percent assessment call limit. No other assessment association in the country could boast of a better record.

The third major concern for the assurance of the Association's continuing success was related to expense. Here too other life insurance companies, both mutual and assessment, might well have looked in awe and envy at Bankers Life record of frugality in operating expenses. Initially, Temple and Simon Casady had each put up $750 of his own money to buy the necessary office supplies until such time as the contingent fund would be able to provide. And for the first two or three years most of the labor was volunteer, unpaid labor, and most of that labor was Simon Casady's. Not only had the Casadys provided rent-free office space for the home office in a back room of their bank, but Simon himself after banking hours did all of the necessary paper work, personally filling out each certificate of membership with a beautifully ornate calligraphy, and balancing the books after each day's transactions. President Temple, after launching his child into the world, had returned to his bank in Chariton, but he made frequent trips to Des Moines, at his own expense, of course, to supervise operations. Until the guarantee deposit fund reached the $100,000 level, no officer or Board director received any salary. Not until 1888, four years after he had moved to Des Moines permanently, following the death of his wife, did Temple begin to get a salary as president of the company, although apparently from the minutes of the Board, he did receive commissions on business solicited. In 1888 his salary was fixed at $3,500 per year plus travel expenses. In 1890 it was raised to $6,000, and even that was very modest as compared to the salaries most life insurance companies paid their presidents at that time.

Increased business by 1882 did force the Association to employ its first paid labor in order to relieve the greatly overburdened Simon Casady. On January 6, 1882, the Board approved of a contract with John A. Tibbs of Des Moines who was to serve as general agent "for all the states in which the Association does business." And when the Board specified "general," it did mean *general*. Tibbs was expected to: (1) solicit new members; (2) select and establish bank depositories; (3) appoint state, local, and traveling solicitors; (4) handle all clerical duties of the Association except for the records of the Board of Directors; (5) keep general supervision over all solicitors; (6) report to the president "not oftener than monthly"; and (7) perform "all other duties in accordance with the constitution and by-laws." For this rather awesome assignment, Tibbs was to keep for himself everything that remained in the contingent fund after all of the following expenses had been paid: (1) wages for a clerk, stationery, office rent, advertising, printing, postage, and expressage; (2) payment to depository banks of 5 percent on the guarantee deposit placed there on application for membership; (3) payment of salary or commissions per contract to state, local, and traveling solicitors; (4) payment of the travel expenses of the Board of Directors including railroad fares; (5) payment for gathering evidence in death loss or in event of lawsuits; and (6) payment of reasonable attorney fees. Considering the amount of money in the contingent fund in 1882, clearly Tibbs was not going to be ruined by affluence. Tibbs's only hope for any compensation whatsoever was to reduce expenses to the barest essentials. Perhaps he was overly zealous in his economy, for in June he was censured by the Board for "certain shortcomings," and was replaced by his recently hired assistant, Nason B. Collins, who soon thereafter became secretary of the Association to replace Simon Casady, who had moved on up to the vice-presidency.

In 1882, the Association moved from the back room of the Des Moines Bank to somewhat larger quarters at 211 Fourth Street, but by 1885 that office could no longer accommodate the business of the Association, so the home office was again moved to a three-room office in the Youngerman Building on Fifth Street. This was the beginning of the home office's peripatetic wanderings that for the next half century would see it moving from one office building to another in the downtown loop area: the Iowa Loan and Trust Building in 1888, the Marquardt Building in 1890, the old Equitable Building (later known as the Bankers Trust Building) in 1896, the Valley National Bank Building in 1917, and finally to the Liberty Building at the corner of Sixth and Grand, where it eventually occupied the top seven floors. No one in those years could accuse Bankers Life of excessive outlay in plant facilities, although its moving costs must have been extraordinary.

Economy remained the key word throughout the thirty years of Temple's presidency. No one was more assiduous in complying with Temple's Spartan code for operating expenses then was A. C. Stilson, who was appointed secretary of the Association in 1889. The stories of Stilson's frugality became legendary within the home office. All office supplies, stationery, pencils, and postage stamps were kept in his office and were carefully guarded. No new pencil would be issued until an old pencil of less than two inches in length was turned in as proof of real need.

For the officers and directors of the Association it was an easy matter for them to practice economy in their business activities, since they so zealously adhered to it in their personal lives. No Terrace Hill ostentatious display for them. Most of them, including the Casadys, lived in quite modest homes within easy walking distance of the business district, and they accounted for every penny of their household expenses with the same vigorous scrutiny that Stilson gave to lead pencils. Dr. F. J. Will of Eagle Grove, who was appointed medical examiner for the Association in 1900, insisted that his son who was in college account for the expenditure of every cent of the allowance given him. One month there remained five cents that was unaccounted for. In reply to his father's demand for an explanation as to what had happened to that nickel, the son wrote back, "Sorry, Dad. I should have added another line in my monthly budget: 5¢—for keeping a woman."

Economy, growth, and the careful selectivity of membership—these were the basic tenets of policy and practice that enabled The Bankers Life Association to continue to flourish while many other assessment companies floundered and ultimately drowned in an ever-rising tide of assessment levies. For thirty years, the basic Temple Plan as established in 1879 remained unchanged, and so did the basic operating procedures. One reason for this constancy in operations was the remarkable stability of officer personnel for over a quarter of a century. Of the original five directors and two additional officers chosen in 1879, only two had a rather brief association with Bankers Life. M. S. Smalley, cashier of the First National Bank in Galesburg, Illinois, resigned within a year to move to California. B. F. Elbert of Albia was in poor health when he joined the Board, and he too resigned early in 1880. Of the remaining five, all remained active in the affairs of the Association for twenty years or more. P. M. Casady, one of Des Moines' first citizens and distinguished jurists and businessmen, resigned from the Board in 1887, but through his son, Simon, who served as his surrogate both as vice-president and director, Judge Casady remained actively interested in the affairs of the Association until his death in 1908. Lyman Cook, president of the First National Bank of Burlington, was the first treasurer and held that office until his death in 1898.

The remaining three original directors and officers were still holding office when the Association celebrated its silver anniversary in 1904. Dr. George Glick, who was born in Germany in 1827 and came to the United States following the Revolution of 1848, tried gold mining in California in 1849 before settling down in Marshalltown, first as a dry-goods merchant and grocer, later as pharmacist, and finally as banker, when he organized the First National Bank of Marshalltown. Although there is no record as to when and if he ever received a medical degree, he always proudly claimed the title of doctor, a not uncommon practice for pharmacists of that day, and he served on the Board of Directors and as medical director for the Association until his death in 1906.

Finally there were Edward Temple and Simon Casady, father and chief nurse of The Bankers Life Association. Simon Casady, born in Des Moines in 1852, always lived in the shadow of his father's great name and fame. The Casadys claimed to be descendants of a Spanish gallant, Casada, who settled in England after the defeat of the Spanish Armada off the coast of Britain in 1588. If true, the Casady line had become thoroughly anglicized, for there was nothing to suggest the fiery, tempestuous Spanish temperament in either P. M.'s or his son Simon's character. First secretary of the Association, later vice-president, financial director, and finally treasurer from 1899 to 1928, Simon Casady held every high office in the Association except that of president. No other man in the history of Bankers Life served on the Board of Directors longer than he. Cautious and conservative, he fully supported Edward Temple's plan and operating procedures and perhaps hoped to be his designated heir apparent.

As the Association continued to grow in membership and wealth, new men were of course brought in as officers, directors, and department heads. One of the most innovative steps taken by Temple during his thirty-year presidency was the hiring of young Henry S. Nollen as the Association's first real actuary in 1893, although his official title was Auditor of Accounts, a newly created position. Nollen was the son of John Nollen of Pella, Iowa, a distinguished mathematics scholar and successful banker, and grandson of Dominie Henry Scholte, who had brought a group of Dutch Pietists over from Holland and had founded the town of Pella in 1847. Young Henry, who had been professor of mathematics at Central College in Pella, came to Des Moines in 1889, where he first found employment with the Citizens National Bank and then as auditor for the United Gas Improvement Company. When he left that company to accept the position with Bankers Life, his former employer generously gave him a two weeks' additional salary. Nollen was quickly apprised of Bankers Life's policy of thrift when after not receiving any pay for two weeks, he mentioned that fact to President Temple. Temple replied gently, "My dear boy, I understand the Gas Company paid you two weeks' salary when you left there to come here. Surely, you don't expect to be paid twice for the same two weeks do you?" And even if Nollen expected it, which he did, he never got it.

In the same year that Nollen joined Bankers Life, the Board of Directors for the first time adopted the Homans American Experience Table of Mortality as a basis for anticipating death claims in advance of the next quarter. This was a small step forward in a more scientific analysis of life contingencies than that which had ever before prevailed within the Association. But the adoption of Homans' table in no way meant a change in the basic rate structure or assessment program of the Temple Plan.

Henry Nollen, self-trained actuary and close student of the mathematical laws of probabilities, must have spent many long hours discussing the ultimate fate of the assessment plan with his former Pella neighbor and present business associate, I. M. Earle, who had joined the law department of Bankers Life one year after Nollen had come to the Association and who would succeed Judge O. B. Ayres as general counsel for the Association in 1902. Nollen could with cold mathematical logic show that ultimately Temple's assessment plan was doomed to failure. No matter how impressive the growth, no matter how rigid the economy, sooner or later the inexorable law of a higher mortality rate for the aging members of the Association would catch up with the 1 percent mortality figure. Then the emergency reserve fund would have to be utilized, and once it was depleted, assessment calls would soar, membership, particularly among the young, who were the most needed, would drop, and the Association would fail.

Earle would agree with Nollen's mathematical arguments, but he in turn would also point out with the lawyer's knowledge of all of the legal intricacies involved, how difficult it would be to try to convert a long-established assessment company into a new mutual legal reserve company.

Then both Nollen and Earle would shake their heads and agree that it was all a foolish argument anyway. The Temple Plan might have hidden flaws within it, but it would stand like the Parthenon as long as the old man, like an ever-watchful Athena, was around to protect it. And the old man showed no indication of leaving. He would come to his office each morning, would confer at length with the faithful Simon, and would then sit at his desk and smile contentedly as he perused the latest reports of additional life insurance in force. The agents in the field continued to push the assessment plan over the straight commercial or mutual life insurance policies. "No necessity for large reserves at Bankers Life. We let you keep the reserves in your own pockets. Only assessment calls at Bankers Life which will not exceed one percent of your insurance coverage. And look here, for the past year, look at these low assessment calls. Why, it's virtually free insurance, man." So the sales pitch went, and so the new membership deposits poured in and the new certificates went out. Twenty-nine million dollars' worth of insurance in force in 1890, more than double that figure three years later, even though 1893 was a depression year, $143 million in 1900, over $200 million in 1904, when the Association celebrated its twenty-fifth anniversary. And so it went. What was there to worry about? But Henry Nollen continued to worry. He sat at his desk, studying his actuarial tables, and waited for the inevitable Day of Judgment.

2/The Association Becomes a Company
1909-1916

The advent of the twentieth century brought few immediate or visible changes to The Bankers Life Association in either its principles or its operating procedures. The guiding tenets of constant growth, of the careful selectivity of membership, and of economy in operating expenses—those tenets that had enabled the Association to prosper for a quarter of a century—still prevailed. Expenses were kept at a minimum: officers' salaries were rarely and then only reluctantly raised. Although residency standards in respect to geographical regions were relaxed, occupational, physical, and moral standards for individual applicants were rigidly adhered to, and new standards were established as modern technology added new occupations to those deemed too hazardous for the company to accept for insurance. To such forbidden categories as those of police officers, military men, railroad switchmen, and saloonkeepers was added a new occupational hazard when John R. Gammeter of Akron, Ohio, was forced to surrender his certificate of membership in the Association because "he has purchased and expects to operate a flying machine." Minimize risk and expenses, maximize growth—this was President Temple's pat answer to those doom and gloom prophets within his own Association who tried to convince him with their actuarial tables that ultimately the assessment plan would have to fail.

It was hard to argue against the statistics of operational success that Temple held in his hand even with the cold logic of actuarial statistics. Nor could one easily dismiss the glowing report that F. W.

27

Withington, an insurance examiner, submitted to the state auditor, B. F. Carroll, in June 1906. The insurance examiner not only gave the Association very high marks upon its financial soundness and its expert management but he commended the company in extravagant terms for its careful selectivity of membership. He presented data to show that the percent of actual mortality was 47.8—less than half of the expected mortality of 10 deaths per 1,000 population. In quite atypical insurance examiner's prose, Withington wrote:

> *These percentages ... indicate a condition of vitality which I believe to be without parallel.... The extremely low death rate and the remarkably small fluctuation [over a twenty-year period] will be noted. I attribute this unusually healthy condition of membership in great part to the extreme care exercised in medical selection by competent and experienced medical examiners, but I believe it to be also due to the system of requiring recommendation of applicants by persons known to be responsible, thus insuring a membership of high quality and minimizing the moral risk. The strict enforcement of the provisions of the policy or certificate relating to temperance is also, in my opinion, a large factor in the production of the results shown above....*

With this kind of mortality rate among its members and with the operating expense factor kept at about one half of that charged by the commercial and legal reserve life insurance companies, it is hardly surprising that Bankers Life could offer a $2,000 certificate with annual assessment calls at less than half of the premiums charged for legal reserve ordinary life. It is true that the Bankers Life certificate paid no dividends and had no cash surrender value, but the accumulated savings over a twenty-year period on premiums offered graphic proof for the Association's claim that it was furnishing "pure, unadulterated life insurance at the smallest net cost to the policyholder ... who can keep the savings and the reserves in his own pocket."

Unfortunately, however, most assessment companies could not present such a remarkable "condition of vitality" as did Bankers Life. Few could be, or would be, as selective in their membership, few had built within their plan any kind of age differential for assessment, and none was able to keep operating expenses at the level established and maintained by Temple, Stilson, and company. As more and more fraternal societies and assessment companies were driven out of business by ever-mounting assessment rates, public concern grew, and this concern was reflected in political action. Bills were introduced in many state legislatures to prohibit the formation of any new assessment companies and to prevent existing companies from soliciting any new business.

The initial response of Bankers Life to these attempts to restrict and regulate assessment companies was to mobilize its own membership to lobby against such proposed bills. The call would go out: "A bill has been introduced in the Ohio legislature which seeks to destroy your Association. Write your state legislator and ask him to vote against it." The membership would respond as one man, like an old marine hearing the order to "Charge the foe." The letters, telegrams, and phone calls would pour in. One beleaguered New York legislator in desperation wrote to the home office in Des Moines, "For God's sake, call off your members. I can't sleep or eat as the phone rings day and night all the time."

One of the most effective organizers against unfavorable state legislation was George Kuhns, who had joined Bankers Life in 1896 as a field agent. Kuhns was born on a farm near Andalusia, Illinois, in 1861. After finishing high school at Edgington, Illinois, he enrolled in 1880 at Iowa State College in Ames, Iowa, where in order to pay for his expenses, he worked at a variety of jobs including labor on road gangs as a substitute for college professors in the payment of their poll taxes. Leaving Iowa State before completing the work for his degree, Kuhns apparently was involved in several real estate promotional schemes prior to finding his proper niche as an insurance salesman. He quickly became one of the top salesmen for Bankers Life, and in 1902 he made his first appearance in the minutes of the Board of Directors meeting with the notation that his salary as Field Manager would be fixed at $3,500 a year. It was as field manager that he won fame within the Association not only for his remarkable sales production records but also for his ability to organize the troops against restrictive legislation in every state in which Bankers Life was authorized to do business. A large, heavy-set man, Kuhns had the power and drive of a steam locomotive, and he had the messianic, oratorical skills of a secular Billy Sunday to inspire his field agents to produce more and more sales. From the moment he arrived in the home office in Des Moines, it was apparent that Kuhns was going to be a dynamic power to be reckoned with.

At the same time that Kuhns and his agents were monthly setting new sales records in their promotion of the superiority of assessment insurance over ordinary life policies, Henry Nollen was working at cross purposes by quietly persuading most of the officers and directors of the Association that if Bankers Life was to survive it must be converted into a mutual legal reserve life insurance company. Even the cautious and conservative Simon Casady was ultimately convinced by Henry's statistics that the assessment plan could not endure forever.

In 1905 the New York state legislature appointed a special committee headed by Assemblyman Armstrong to make a thorough investigation into the alleged corrupt practices of some of the nation's largest insurance companies, assessment, stock, and mutual, which were either based in or doing business in the state of New York. When the very thoroughly documented Armstrong report was released in 1906, the public outcry for remedial legislation could not be ignored. Further impetus was given to the reform movement in 1907 when the Mutual Reserve Fund Association, which had once been the country's largest assessment company, failed after trying belatedly and unsuccessfully to convert itself into a legal reserve company. The failure of the Mutual Association, which in 1896 had had over $325 million worth of insurance in force, convinced Nollen and his colleagues that Bankers Life must convert before waiting too long, as Mutual had done.

But Temple remained adamant in his opposition to change. He could point out that Mutual had failed because it had not built into its assessments the age of entry factor, it had not been careful in its selection of members, and above all, it had been extravagant in its expenses. Temple could point to one item in the Armstrong report that offered clear and damning evidence as to why Mutual was bound to fail—$30,000 for chartering a yacht to entertain the New York State insurance commissioners. Compare that to Bankers Life's two-inch pencils and you will understand the difference between the two companies, Temple argued.

Quite obviously, there would be no action on conversion as long as Temple was on the scene. Henry Nollen, however, continued to prepare for the inevitable. While Kuhns, backed by Temple, was organizing his agents and their customers against restrictive legislation elsewhere, Nollen and Earle were doing a quite different kind of lobbying in their own home state legislature. With the behind-the-scenes counsel of these two men, a House committee reported out and the Iowa General Assembly passed a bill in 1907 that authorized any assessment company incorporated within the state to convert into a legal reserve company and to put a new legal reserve plan into effect, subject to the approval of the Iowa insurance commissioner. Nollen and Earle now had the law as well as the future on their side.

At the meeting of the Board of Directors on July 10, 1907, President Temple cast the sole dissenting vote against the raising of the salary for his vice-president, Ernest E. Clark, to $6,000 and again was alone in opposing a salary increase to $6,000 for the Association's secretary, Henry Nollen. But significantly he offered no opposition to increasing the salary of his field manager, George Kuhns, to the same $6,000 level. All of these presidential actions must have been duly noted, if not openly commented upon, by the parties most directly concerned. Clearly a struggle for power was in the making and the lines were being drawn. Kuhns was now openly allied with Temple in opposition to Clark, Nollen, and Earle. Critical to both factions was the state of President Temple's health. If the founder of the Association could survive a few more years, Kuhns expected to be firmly entrenched in power. For Nollen and Earle, the question was not so much their own positions within the company—although that was a matter of no small interest to them—but more important, would Temple hold on to the assessment plan beyond the time when it would be possible to successfully convert the Association into a mutual legal reserve company?

By the fall of 1908 it was apparent that Temple's health was failing. In December he attended his last Board meeting and then headed south to Orlando, Florida, in the hopes that a winter of Florida sunshine would restore him to health. In February the home office received notice that it must now pay out the death benefit for Certificate No. 1. On February 12, 1909, at the age of seventy-seven, Edward A. Temple died. The Board met on February 16 and passed the following motion:

> *Resolved, that in the death of Edward A. Temple, the individual members of the Board of Directors suffer the loss of a valuable friend and counselor and the Association, a most faithful and deserving official. As the founder and President since its formation, he has left for himself in this Association an enduring monument. To its interests he devoted his increasing energies, and the care with which it has been managed was largely due to his persistent vigilance.*

An era had ended. In thirty years, Temple had seen his "quiet, insignificant child" grow into a $400 million giant, the largest and most successful assessment company in America, doing business in twenty-five states, Canada, and the District of Columbia. No one could question the Board's statement that with his departure Temple had left behind an impressive monument. But how enduring that monument would be was quite a different question.

One week later, the Board of Directors met to select Temple's successor. The choice was an obvious one both logically and politically. Vice-President Clark was unanimously elected as the second president of the Association. It was a clear victory for Nollen, who had been assured by Clark that he was sympathetic toward Nollen's proposal for conversion.

Nollen and Earle at once began working in earnest to convert the Association into a mutual legal reserve company. Rate schedules were established, legal procedures were designed, promotional campaigns were discussed. All of these plans were developed in secret. There is no indication in the Board minutes that the subject of conversion was ever formally on the agenda for discussion at any time during the next two years.

As to how much George Kuhns knew about these initial plans for conversion, it is difficult to say. He continued to push his agents to stress the advantages of assessment certificates over ordinary life insurance policies. And he continued to get results. By 1911 Bankers Life Association had nearly half a billion dollars' worth of insurance in force. To all reported rumors that the Association, fearing the fate of the Mutual Association, was considering conversion, he had just one stock answer: "It's a damned lie."

Kuhns must have realized, however, that his own position within the inner circle of power was in serious jeopardy with the departure of Temple. Clark personally represented no direct threat. A quiet, unassuming, gentle man, Clark had no deep commitments he would battle for. It is ironic that this rather ineffective and quite unaggressive man should be the one who was destined to preside over the most momentous single era in the company's history.

However diffident and unassuming Clark may have been, Kuhns still had to reckon with the fact that Clark was president and that he was openly allied with Nollen. So also were Casady and Earle. Indeed, of the five directors, only Dr. F. J. Will, the medical director who was elected to the Board of Directors to succeed Temple, was as yet uncommitted. The odds were heavily against Kuhns, but he was a fighter and as adept in selling himself as he was in selling insurance.

By the spring of 1911 Nollen and Earle had completed their plans for conversion. The Board minutes for this period are extremely sparse and give no indication of any discussion of these plans, but surely there must have been open discussion among the directors and officers of the company as to when these plans should be announced and implemented. Although not a member of the Board, Kuhns as one of the eight officers of the Association must have been privy to these discussions. Kuhns, to be sure, had been Temple's staunchest ally in opposing any suggestion for conversion, but now Temple was dead, and Kuhns, as always, was a supreme realist. To oppose conversion now would be not only futile but also suicidal. Kuhns asked only that he be allowed in his own way and at his own time to prepare his loyal field force for the inevitable. As a first step, on May 17, 1911, he sent out a letter to all of his agents informing them that hereafter they would receive a commission not only for new business obtained but also for renewals—something that the Association, unlike most other insurance companies, had never done. Clearly Kuhns was attempting to coat the bitter pill the agents would soon have to swallow with a little sugar in the hopes that they would not gag and refuse to take it.

In the same month of May, a New York actuary, S. J. Wolfe, was employed to audit the Association's books, a necessary initial requirement under Iowa law for conversion. When Wolfe completed his audit and submitted his report in September, an insurance trade journal, *The New York Independent*, picked up this small news item and at once deduced what was happening. It published a story reporting that Bankers Life had just concluded a special audit by an outside actuary. "Is not this a preliminary step to conversion?" the journal speculated. Kuhns immediately began to get worried inquiries from some of his agents to which he promptly sent back his familiar stock answer: "You may say to anyone who asks you that the 'rumor' is unfounded and that the question has never been acted upon by the Board. ... You should pay no attention to what is published in the *Independent* or anything that is inspired by it."

Kuhns may have been straining the truth a bit, but he was not actually lying to his agents. The Board had not taken any official action as yet, but it could hardly delay the proceedings much longer.

On October 12, 1911, two letters were sent out to all field agents of the Association. The first was written by Kuhns:

To All Agents:
The agents of competing companies are busy circulating a report which emanated from a hostile insurance journal published in New York. You may say to any of our policyholders or prospective applicants that the statement that this Company is going to change its members over to the old line basis is absolutely false. No change whatever is to be made in their contracts and the statement that liens will be placed against their policies and their rates raised to old line rates is a lie pure and simple.

> *The Bankers Life Association*
> *By Kuhns*

Again, it is necessary to read this letter very carefully to find the grain of truth within it. Kuhns does not say that the Association will not convert itself into a mutual reserve company. All he is saying is that existing assessment contracts will continue to be honored. The impression he creates for the hasty reader, however, is quite different.

On the same day, another letter addressed "To All Agents" was sent out by the home office with no single authorship indicated. It created quite a different impression:

For some time we have had in mind doing away with the guarantee note and membership fee and making a flat rate, just so much a thousand per year. Under the present arrangement a great deal of misunderstanding arises from the fact that the first payment does not cover the insurance for a full twelve months' period. Our present policy is issued and accepted as a quarterly renewable term contract without any guarantee as to what the rate will be and with no rate stated. Within thirty days we shall issue in place of the present policy a renewable term policy with a stated rate guaranteed for ten years. The rate is scientifically constructed, and each year, beginning at the end of the second year, the savings will remain to the credit of the policyholder and be applied to reduce his succeeding premium payments. On the enclosed card you will find a table of rates.

There was only one way in which to read this letter. Clearly, The Bankers Life Association was going to cease selling assessment memberships and was going to offer hereafter only old-line life insurance policies. Receiving both of these letters in the same mail must have thrown the entire field force into utter confusion and consternation. What was happening in Des Moines? How do you reconcile Kuhns's letter with the second letter? Was the Association converting itself within thirty days into a legal reserve company or wasn't it?

The agents did not have long to wait for an answer. On October 26, 1911, the Board finally took formal action. It adopted amended Articles of Incorporation and By-Laws "... so as to transform it [The Bankers Life Association] into a level premium life insurance company under Section 1798b, Supplement of 1907 to the Code of Iowa, operating on the Mutual plan...." On the following day, these amended Articles of Incorporation were filed with the Polk County recorder and the Secretary of State of Iowa. So it was done. The Bankers Life Association had become the Bankers Life Company by formal legal action. Now all that was necessary was to convince the agents, the members, and the general public that the transformation had been both necessary and wise. That promised to be no small task.

First, it was essential to convince the agents. A special task force was created. C. C. Blevins was employed "for special work at a salary not to exceed four hundred and twenty dollars a month and traveling expenses, for such a period as may be deemed necessary and not exceeding one year." And Blevins' traveling expenses were not insignificant. It was his task to hold a series of meetings throughout the Midwest and East in which all of the agents in a particular territory were assembled for an elaborate dinner and were then given a high-powered sales talk on why ordinary life was better than the old assessment. Blevins must have had the courage of Daniel, for it was no easy task to enter these many lion dens and try to convince the assembled group that what they had been extolling for years was now inferior to what they had been so successfully damning. The world for these agents had been turned upside down—bad had suddenly become good, good had become bad. It was hard to take, and many of the agents walked out in disgust. But Blevins had been carefully coached by Kuhns. His oratory was mellifluous, his reasoning sound, and above all, the inducements he had to offer were most enticing— higher commissions on new business, renewal commissions, and especially, commissions up to 50 percent of the premiums paid by those assessment members who could be induced to convert their certificates into the new level premium policies. Clearly the days of Stilson and Temple were over, and expenses were going to be considerably higher.

Clinton L. Booth, a successful field agent in Ohio, was brought into the home office as part of the conversion task force with the title of Superintendent of Agencies. His task was to organize and direct Blevins' field meetings, to answer direct inquiries from agents in the field, and in general, to promote the new level premium policy line in whatever ways he could devise.

As had been true for the Association in its beginnings, so now also for the newly organized company, individual bankers were to be key figures in its initial success. Agents were instructed to call first on the bankers in each town in which there were assessment members. Get the banker to agree to convert his certificate into a new policy and then spread the word among the local members that their banker had converted and that they should do the same. In many instances, it was not difficult to persuade the banker of the wisdom of the change. With Nollen's statistics to reinforce his own arguments, the agent could convince the banker that although the assessment rates were now very low, they would ultimately have to rise to prohibitive heights, once the reserve fund was depleted. For many bankers, with some vague understanding of actuarial tables, these arguments made sense, and they readily agreed to the conversion.

A few agents, however, in their zeal to convince recalcitrant bankers and with their main concern for the lucrative commissions they themselves would receive, tried to use a more powerful and tangible persuasion than Nollen's statistics. One angry banker testified under oath: "I, Merlin P. Resch, Cashier of Benton Harbor State Bank, do hereby state under oath, that I was on or about August 10, 1914, offered by Mr. Hook, Jr., of Detroit, Michigan, representing The Bankers Life Company of Des Moines, the sum of thirty-five ($35.00) dollars, if I would change my policy in the Bankers Life Co., of Des Moines, from the Natural Premium Plan to the Legal Reserve Plan, and give him a letter to that effect. And also I should receive $10.00 on every policy in this City, changed from the old Assessment or Natural Premium Plan, to the Legal Reserve Plan, as an additional remuneration for said letter." Needless to say, such tactics were not condoned by the home office. How often they were used by some individual agents it is difficult to say.

The real responsibility for selling the agents, the members, and the public on Bankers Life's new products fell, of course, on George

Kuhns. He probably never before or after in his busy, energetic life worked as hard as he did during these crucial years of transition. "Convert as many old members as you can, sell as many new policies as you can—go, go, go." This was the pep talk he repeated over and over again to his field force. With the unhappy experience of the Mutual Association constantly in their minds, of remembering how that assessment company had dropped from a high of $325 million of insurance in force in 1896 to a low after that company converted of $77 million in 1906, at which time it folded, the officers and directors of Bankers Life depended on Kuhns's salesmanship for not allowing that to happen to them.

Kuhns told the Board that if the company was going to survive it needed some truly new products. One could not expect even his best salesmen—and there were none better—to compete successfully with the old established legal reserve companies selling the same old ordinary life, particularly when these companies were using scare techniques, warning prospective customers that Bankers Life premiums were always going to be higher than theirs because Bankers Life had thousands of old assessment members whom they would have to carry along for years.

To meet this need for new products, Henry Nollen in January 1912 enticed his younger brother, Gerard, away from Equitable Life of Iowa, where he had already established a name for himself as a promising young actuary. Gerard Nollen was the youngest of the five brilliant children of John and Johanna Scholte Nollen of Pella. Educated at Grinnell College, young Gerard had early shown the same genius for mathematics as that of his father and brother Henry. His task upon coming to Bankers Life was to develop policies that would be new and attractive to the public. Within a few months he had given to the sales force two new policies, with premium rates based on somewhat different calculations than those used by most of the large eastern companies. As Edmund M. McConney, who was to succeed Gerard Nollen as chief actuary and later as president, wrote in his *Reminiscences of Bankers Life*:

> The big mutual companies, after the Armstrong Investigation, were basing their premiums for Ordinary Life policies, then the most popular type of policy, on the American Experience Table of Mortality with 3% interest and an expense element of 33⅓%. Gerard Nollen, knowing that interest rates in the Mid-West were higher than in the East, decided that he would use

3½% interest rate; and with Bankers Life history of strict expense control, decided to use an expense element of 25% with the same table of mortality. He then produced the famous "Life Paid Up at Seventy" policy which was to become so popular in the following years that over 70% of the new level premium business issued by Bankers Life was on this form. It was a major factor in the successful transition from assessment insurance in the Company.

There were two very important sales advantages in this policy:

1. *At the younger and middle ages, the premium rates were lower than the Ordinary Life rates of the big companies.*
2. *Salesmen were not slow in pointing out to prospects that in an Ordinary Life policy one might have to pay to age 96 (the end of the table) if he lived so long, but in the Bankers Life he would be paid up at age 70 thereby saving 26 years premiums. It sold a lot of business.*

Mr. Nollen also developed the Semi-Endowment policy at age 70. This policy provided protection to age 70 and then at that age matured for one-half its face amount. The rate for this was also quite low and it was sold readily.

In addition to obtaining Gerard Nollen's new policies to sell, Kuhns enlarged the potential market in 1912 by persuading the Board to offer insurance to males as young as fifteen years and for the first time in Bankers Life history, to offer insurance to women, who had previously been excluded because Temple always regarded childbearing as being too dangerous an occupation to warrant membership. Even with these innovations, and in spite of the aggressiveness of his hardworking sales force, Kuhns was in serious trouble with sales. Three years after the conversion, of the 245,000 certificates in force with the Association in 1911, 195,000 still remained in force. Approximately a third of the 50,000 certificates lost had been those that had been successfully converted into new level premium policies, but two thirds of the lost certificates represented those who had allowed their membership to lapse without converting to new policies. The total insurance in force had dropped from $490 million to $406 million. This was not the precipitous decline that the Mutual Association had suffered and that had led to its failure, but certainly it was enough of a decline to keep George Kuhns from relaxing.

The first year after conversion was also critical for the future of the company because of the contest for power between Kuhns and Henry Nollen—the only really bitter internecine struggle in the company's history.

Nollen had entered that contest with everything seemingly favoring him. It had been he who had consistently urged conversion and who had with great skill and industry worked out the proper plans. He had at least four fifths of the Board's support. Moreover, in spite of their philosophic differences, Nollen and Temple were of the same character, men of integrity and probity, conservative and temperate in behavior and taste. More intelligent and innovative than Temple, far more aggressive than Clark, Nollen nevertheless would have maintained the tradition of Bankers Life presidencies that the first two chief executive officers had established.

Kuhns had none of these advantages. Emerging out of a poverty-stricken and somewhat shadowy past, he lacked the style and grace of a nineteenth-century gentleman. Rumors of his wheeling-and-dealing promotions bothered his fellow officers in the company, and his overweening ambition repelled men like Clark, Casady, and Nollen. But Kuhns had one advantage that Nollen lacked. He had been hungry all of his life—hungry for the simple necessities of life as a child, hungry for money as a young man, hungry for power as a mature adult. Hunger teaches the bright boy how to survive and how to win. Kuhns had learned a lot about both from his cruel teacher. Nollen was at least as bright as Kuhns, but he had never hungered for anything. He never wanted anything as badly as Kuhns wanted everything. Consequently, the odds for this contest were actually in Kuhns's favor.

Kuhns's first move was to attack the weak points in Nollen's existing Board of Directors. Clark and Casady, of course, were solidly behind Nollen. But Will was rather quickly won over to Kuhns's side. Then, to Nollen's utter amazement, Earle changed sides. Earle and Nollen were old friends and neighbors in Pella. They had worked closely together for years in the Association, and together they had formulated the whole plan for conversion. Nollen must have felt closer to Earle than to any other officer in the company. But Earle, like Kuhns, was a realist. He was fully aware of the great hazards Bankers Life faced in its attempted conversion. Nollen could formulate the plan that had all of the preciseness and beauty of an Euclidean mathematical theorem, but now a Kuhns was necessary to execute the plan successfully. If Bankers Life was going to succeed in the intense competitive struggle that was the world of the insurance business, then it would take all of the aggression, push, and drive that Kuhns manifested in such extraordinary measure. So Earle allied himself with Kuhns.

Having won over two of the five directors, Kuhns then took full advantage of a change in the Articles of Incorporation which he may have been responsible for. The amended Articles that converted the Association into the Bankers Life Company had increased the Board of Directors from five to seven. Kuhns was determined to control those two appointments. One of the two directorships should go to him, a point that even the Nollen-controlled Board was willing to concede. But Clark and Nollen were determined that the other director would be a man of their own choosing. Thus they would still have control of the Board by a four-to-three margin. Kuhns, by hook or by crook, had to secure both nominations if he was to succeed.

The Board meeting in March 1912 duly nominated George Kuhns and Clinton L. Booth for election to the Board of Directors and E. E. Clark for reelection. Ballots were prepared bearing those three names and instructing all policyholders to vote for three directors. Booth, who had been brought in as superintendent of agencies during the period of conversion the previous fall, had quickly allied himself with Nollen, and both Nollen and Clark had seen him as a possible replacement for Kuhns if and when it should be necessary to get rid of Kuhns. Kuhns knew that with the election of Booth, which should automatically follow, his future within the company would be limited. With the stakes this high, he was prepared to fight back in a manner that Nollen and Clark, with their old-school morality and honor, could not even imagine.

A night or two after the official ballots had been mailed, two of Kuhns's allies, who happily were employed in the printing office, worked far into the night. They printed up a new set of ballots containing three names: E. E. Clark, George Kuhns, and W. O. Finkbine. These ballots, unlike all other ballots in the past, were printed on postage-paid cards, with instructions to the policyholders to vote for three directors and then simply drop the card in a mailbox.

Kuhns mailed a supply of these second ballots along with a letter marked confidential to all of the hundreds of agents in the field who were faithfully loyal to him. He recalled for them all that he had done for them in the past and all that he hoped to do for them in the future:

I mention this only to say that if you appreciate the effort that has been made for the welfare of the agents, and will follow my lead in the election of the new directors that takes place the ninth of April ... it will be necessary to leave Mr. Booth temporarily off the Board of Directors. ... Mr. Booth is an able assistant ... and a splendid man ... but he is in no position to assert his opinions in opposition to the opinions of the "powers that be," hence it takes a stronger man on the Board to gain the desired end at this time.

Follow my lead and you win. What I want you to do is to call upon all the Bankers Life members that you can before the 9th of April and see that they send in the ballot herewith enclosed instead of the one that went out with Mr. Booth's name on it ... I need all the votes I can get for myself and Mr. Finkbine. ... Am covering the entire field in this matter and if each man does his part the point will be gained. Have sent you a supply of ballots, postage paid under a separate cover; if you run out, work over some of those sent out with the call and be sure Finkbine's name is written on them.

In answering this letter please used the enclosed envelope which has my residence address on it. Get word to as many of your agents as are handy and be sure the voter puts his policy number after his signature.

If you believe "God helps those who help themselves," get busy and treat this in strict confidence. Gather up the ballots as you go along and mail them yourself so they will reach Des Moines Sunday, the 7th of April. ... Don't leave the impression with the policyholder that there is any contest on.

On April 16 the Board proceeded to canvass the votes. Nollen and Clark, who like the policyholders were blissfully unaware that there was "any contest on," were dumbfounded by the results. Clark, whose name appeared on both ballots, received 35,278 votes. Kuhns, who also was on both ballots, received 35,377 votes. But the official nominee, Booth, received only 13,552 votes while Finkbine, who as far as Clark and Nollen knew had appeared from nowhere, received 21,842 votes. Resolution No. 5167 declared Messrs. Clark, Kuhns, and Finkbine elected to the Board. The loyalty of the agents to Kuhns and the prepaid one-cent ballot cards had paid off handsomely. Kuhns was now in control of the Board.

Kuhns took immediate advantage of his power. On April 17, the day after the votes had been canvassed, he took his seat on the

Board and at once made a motion to create a new office—that of second vice-president, "to have general supervision of the field work and agency force and all that pertains thereto." By a vote of 4–3, the motion carried. Vice-President Earle then moved that Kuhns be elected second vice-president. This motion carried by the same vote. There would be no question now about Kuhns's being in a superior position to Booth over the field force. Indeed, he would no longer be accountable even to President Clark in his control of the agents.

Finkbine, who owed his initial election to the Board to this rather unusual and highly suspect procedure, was a lawyer and wealthy lumberman from Odebolt, Iowa. As the first director ever to be elected from outside the company's own officers, Finkbine, in spite of the impropriety of his initial election, proved to be an able and effective director, serving for eighteen years until his death in 1930.

Henry Nollen made one last attempt in December 1912 to wrest power away from Kuhns. Knowing that Will was in poor health and wished to retire from the Board, Nollen proposed that Clinton L. Booth be substituted as a nominee for the Board in place of Will for the next election to the Board. This motion, however, was defeated 4–3, with Clark, Nollen and Casady in the minority. One week later, Will announced his retirement from the Board. Kuhns immediately nominated another outsider, a Des Moines lawyer by the name of Clinton L. Nourse. The fact that Kuhns's nominee had the same first name and middle initial as the "Clinton L." whom Nollen had wanted was a nice bit of insult to add to the injury—a point that was not lost on Nollen. Clinton L. Nourse was nominated instead of Clinton L. Booth by a 4–2 vote. (Casady was absent.)

Henry Nollen had at last had enough. On December 24 he submitted his resignation from the Board and from the company he had served so well in order to accept the vice-presidency at Equitable Life of Iowa. Kuhns's triumph was complete. Henry Nollen could never forget nor forgive the manner in which he had been defeated. Years later when testifying in a court suit involving Bankers Life's conversion he was asked about the role of George Kuhns in that transitional period, Nollen drew himself up straight and with a grim face snapped out a one-sentence reply: "Mr. Kuhns assumed all authority."

And so Kuhns had. But George Kuhns in victory could be more magnanimous than Henry Nollen in defeat. As soon as Nollen's resignation was accepted by the Board at the December 24 meeting, Kuhns moved that Henry be replaced on the Board and as secretary of the company by Gerard Nollen. It was a nice gesture of conciliation, acceptable to Gerard if not to Henry. Moreover, it ensured for Kuhns and the company a continuation of the Nollen mathematical aptitude and managerial ability. Gerard Nollen, in turn, remained faithful in his loyalty to Kuhns. Years later when he wrote his *Historical Sketch of the Bankers Life Company*, he made no mention of the struggle that drove his brother out of the company. Of Kuhns, Gerard Nollen wrote, "He was an able leader of men." Not even Henry Nollen could question that.

On April 18, 1916, President Clark offered his resignation from the presidency and the Board for reasons of ill health, to take effect on July 1. Two days after this announcement, the Board unanimously elected George Kuhns president, and thus was his assumption of "all authority" formally recognized.

3/George Kuhns–
The Field Agents' President

1916-1926

George Kuhns, who became the third president of Bankers Life on July 1, 1916, in his personal background and in his previous experience within the company was unlike any other president the company has had in its one hundred years of existence. He had come out of the field force and he remained a salesman all of his life. Even more significant, he differed from all of his predecessors and successors in his manners and in his methods of operations. Ruthlessly aggressive by nature, he was prepared to fight hard to get what he wanted for himself and for his company, and both he and the company were to benefit by his mode of operations. One of his successors to the presidency, Edmund McConney, who was not at all hesitant in emphasizing Kuhns's strong-arm tactics, nevertheless stated flatly in his Reminiscences *that George Kuhns was the "right man for the right time" in the company's history.*

Bankers Life needed the aggressive leadership of a George Kuhns if it was to escape the fate that had befallen the Mutual Association in its effort to convert from an assessment association into a mutual legal reserve company a decade before. In 1915 the amount of insurance in force with Bankers Life had dropped to $398 million, a hundred-million-dollar loss since 1911, the year that the assessment plan was abandoned. In the first half year of his presidency, Kuhns reversed the trend and increased the insurance in force to $415 million. From that moment on the direction was steadily upward so that within a decade, the amount of insurance Bankers Life had in force more than doubled—to $844 million by 1925 and $909 million in 1926. The admitted assets of the company, which had never shown a decline even during the difficult first years after conversion, also increased at a reassuring rate: $17 million in 1911, $30 million in 1916, $90 million in 1926. George Kuhns knew how to sell insurance, and he saw to it that the premium income was properly invested so as to increase the company's assets. McConney's judgment of him was quite correct.

During the first year as president, Kuhns conducted a strenuous campaign to get the old assessment members to exchange their certificates for new mutual life insurance policies. He created a so-called flying squadron, a group of his top salesmen from the field that included Gene Burke and William Jaeger, to go from one agency city to another to encourage the agents in that area to give major attention to conversion. And Kuhns made the process of conversion as simple as possible for the certificate holder and as remunerative as possible for the agent. One could exchange the old certificate for an equal amount of ordinary life or endowment policy without having to take a physical examination and certainly without any banker's report on one's personal habits. Slowly, the number of certificates outstanding were whittled away: $371 million outstanding in 1913 down to $270 million in 1917, but unfortunately a large percentage of this loss represented not conversion to new policies but simply the lapsing of the certificates by disgruntled former Association members. After a year and a half of this campaign to convert certificates, Kuhns made no further effort. It was clear that the future health of the company was dependent not upon converting old certificates but in selling new policies. And new sales was George Kuhns's special forte.

To achieve the growth needed, Kuhns was quite willing to drop the old standards for the selectivity of members that Temple had insisted upon. As early as 1915, once he had control of the Board, he got a resolution passed that removed all restrictions in future policies in respect to residency, travel, and occupation, with the exception of military and naval service. Policemen, railroad switchmen, even saloonkeepers who might be inclined to sample their own goods were now welcome to apply for insurance with Bankers Life. The limit on the amount of insurance any one individual could take with the company was also drastically raised—from the old limit of $6,000 to $40,000. What Simon Casady, the only surviving proponent of Temple's standards, may have thought of these changes is not a matter of record. Nor would it have made much difference if Casady had entered a formal protest to these changes. Kuhns was out to sell insurance, not to preach temperance or to be a moral arbiter for the nation, and Kuhns controlled the company.

At the turn of the century, the old Bankers Life Association was authorized to do business in twenty-one states. During the next twenty-five years, the company entered fourteen additional states and the District of Columbia. Of all of Temple's strict regulations regarding the selectivity of members, the only one that seemed to survive through the Kuhns era was that of refusing to do business in the Deep South. Although the Board in 1909 opened negotiations to do business in Arkansas and twelve years later approved of the company's entering Georgia, nothing seems to have come of these early efforts of Kuhns to penetrate the land of the old Confederacy. It would not be until the 1940s and 1950s that Bankers Life would seek business in Dixieland. Similarly, the company discreetly stayed out of the six New England states. Apparently, it did not feel strong enough to compete with the giant insurance companies of Hartford and Boston in their home territory. But with these regional exceptions, all of the United States was now the Bankers Life's market.

Kuhns, as president, attempted to bring some kind of systematic order out of the rather haphazard agency sales force that had developed almost without planning during the Temple and Clark regimes. Formal annual contractual relationships were established with sixty-five general agencies. These sixty-five agency centers were generally located in the major cities (New York, Chicago, Los Angeles, San Francisco, and Pittsburgh, for example), but some were in relatively small towns: Terrell, Texas; Fort Dodge, Iowa; Chippewa Falls, Wisconsin; Twin Falls, Idaho; and Salina, Kansas. The general agent in each of these locations, in turn, entered into contractual relations with scores of field agents or salesmen who did most of the actual door-to-door selling. By 1925 there were some three thousand men selling Bankers Life insurance on a full-time or part-time basis. A great deal of this selling was not in the large metropolitan centers, even though the general agent's office might be located there, but out in the small towns and farmlands that surrounded the agency city. Bankers Life continued to remain committed to its own rural origins and aggressively sought its customers as it had in the days of the Association among farmers and small-town merchants, bankers, and tradesmen. The field agent in his Model T Ford, Oldsmobile, or Dodge would travel the deeply rutted roads of Iowa, the dusty plains of the Dakotas, or the sand hills of western Nebraska to spread the gospel of insurance and to make sure that not a single farmer in his territory, no matter how isolated he might be, should go unnoticed, and, it was to be hoped, unsold.

At a meeting of the Board of Directors on November 5, 1918, on a motion by C. L. Nourse, who usually served as Kuhns's spokesman on the Board by introducing those motions that Kuhns wanted passed, the country was divided into five regional districts. The general agents in each region would thereafter be known as agency managers and would be under the supervision of a regional sales manager who in turn would report to a general sales manager at the home office. It was an elaborate superstructure, more impressive on organizational charts than it was effective in actual operations. Many of the former general agents, much as they admired George Kuhns, resented the change in title, for "agency manager" did not connote the same degree of autonomy and independence that the old name, "general agent," implied.

At the top of his hierarchy, the Board created the office of General Sales Manager, and for this position, upon Kuhns's recommendation, the Board appointed E. W. Nothstine, one of the most colorful and certainly the most suspect character in the company's history. Nothstine's early career before becoming associated with Bankers Life is far more obscure and shadowy than even that of George Kuhns. One gets the impression from the vague rumors that forever floated around his name that as soon as Nothstine could walk and talk, he must have been busily engaged in making quick deals, for he was the kind of baby who could take candy away from an adult.

Sometime in the course of his early career of promoting get-rich-quick schemes, he must have met Kuhns. And between the two there very quickly developed a curious kind of liaison, even a brotherly affection, which none of Kuhns's associates at Bankers Life could ever fully understand. Kuhns must have appreciated Nothstine's quick wit, his ingratiating charm, and above all, his remarkable ability to sell anything to anybody. Nothstine, in turn, saw in Kuhns a potentially powerful patron. He was only too happy to hitch his wagon to Kuhns's rapidly rising star. How many various land promotional schemes they may have engaged in together prior to Kuhns's assuming the top position at Bankers Life is impossible to determine. It is a matter of record that both were deeply involved in a Minnesota land operation, the Red Clover Land Company, capitalized at $400,000. Kuhns was president and Nothstine the promotional agent of this company at the time that Kuhns became superintendent of agencies in 1910.

It is quite appropriate to the man that Nothstine should make his first appearance in the minutes of the Bankers Life Board of Directors meeting as an unsuccessful applicant for a real estate loan on a farm he owned in Missouri in December 1913. Simon Casady had moved that the loan be denied and the Board had agreed. Undaunted by this initial rebuff and undoubtedly given encouragement and help by Vice-President Kuhns, Nothstine reappears in the minutes just six weeks later with the simple notation that on a motion by Vice-President Earle the Board agreed to hire E. W. Nothstine for agency work at a salary of $5,000 per annum. From then on, his rise in the company was rapid. Given the agency in San Francisco, he and his subagents sold a lot of insurance, but he was overly generous in extending credit in order to make the sales. In October 1918 the Board for the first time in the company's history, and probably only then at the insistence of Kuhns, passed a motion offered by the faithful Nourse to write off as uncollectible $59,399 of agents' balances. Of the eleven agents involved, Nothstine's uncollected balance represented the lion's share—$37,189.

This financial embarrassment apparently had no detrimental effect upon his future with Bankers Life, however, for in the following month, Nothstine was appointed general sales manager at a salary of $10,000—the same as that given to Vice-President Gerard Nollen. Although in respect to both title and salary Nothstine was now within the top echelon of the company, Kuhns curiously enough never proposed that Nothstine be officially made an executive officer of the company. He was simply to do what he knew how to do best, promote sales by finding new aggressive agents and by inspiring the entire sales force from the five regional sales managers on down to the most temporary, part-time subagent to greater efforts on behalf of the company.

The five regional sales managers appointed in 1918, William Jaeger, R. G. Hake, W. H. North, E. G. Squires, and O. B. Jackman, were nominally under Nothstine and took their traveling orders from him, but they were also, by the Board's direction, under the direct supervision of President Kuhns. They were to visit all of the agencies within their region on a periodic basis to check on how well each agency manager was producing and to recommend changes in personnel as needed. All five men had been successful agents themselves. They would be able to evaluate the effectiveness of any agency manager and to spot trouble before it became serious. Of the five, Jaeger was clearly the most outstanding. Nothstine was a shrewd judge of character, and it did not take him long to see that Jaeger had great potential for leadership. He was the kind of man who could enter a room filled with strangers and immediately command respect and attention. He was bright, forceful, and ambitious. More than any other man in the entire sales organization, Jaeger represented a direct threat to Nothstine's own somewhat tenuous position within the company.

Since Jaeger was under the direct supervision of Kuhns, and Kuhns could clearly see for himself how effective Jaeger was, it was impossible for Nothstine simply to dismiss Jaeger. His only viable recourse was to make conditions so uncomfortable for Jaeger that the latter would leave of his own volition. Nothstine knew that Jaeger was devoted to his wife and that since the death of their only child, a little girl, a couple of years previously, Jaeger never traveled anywhere without taking his wife with him at their own, not the company's, expense. So Nothstine informed Jaeger that inasmuch as he had proved so effective as regional sales manager, hereafter he would be a special troubleshooter for the entire country. Jaeger then began to get orders from Nothstine that took him back and forth across the country, from San Francisco to New York to Texas to Washington state. Thus did Nothstine hope to wear Jaeger out and bankrupt him in the process. It did not take Jaeger long, however, to see what the game was. He protested directly to Kuhns, who told him that hereafter he could stay within his own eastern region.

The attention that Kuhns gave to the organization of the sales force was indicative of the great love he had for selling and for the men who did the selling. Within the home office, he was rather cold, distant, and aloof. Except for Nothstine, among the home office personnel he had no close associates and no one ever called him George. Out in the field, however, he was a different person. He knew all of the agency managers and many of the subagents by their first names. And although they were always respectfully deferential to him, they knew that in George Kuhns they had a true field agents' president. When in his bid for power in 1912 he had sent out a confidential letter in which he had said, "Follow my lead and you win," the agents had willingly followed his lead. Most of them now could feel that they had indeed won. Kuhns's major concern in addressing his sales force was always "How can I help you to sell more insurance?" And he answered his own question in a variety of imaginative ways that could only gratify his salesmen.

He remembered, for instance, his own days in the field and how pitifully little promotional material the home office had provided the sales force and, except for the modest commissions, what few incentives were offered for greater sales production. He was determined to remedy those situations. While still vice-president in 1914, Kuhns began the task of building an effective publications and advertising department. As a first step, he employed Bert N. Mills, the former city editor of the *Des Moines Capital*, the city's leading evening newspaper. Kuhns had been impressed by the fact that of all the local reporters who over the years had done interviews with Bankers Life officers, young Mills's stories, while not necessarily the most flattering, were always the most accurate. He told Mills that he could, in effect, write his own ticket, but what the company needed was communication between the home office and the field. The men out there needed to know what policy changes the home office was considering, what new products the actuaries were developing. They needed to know who their own officers were and what made them tick. Above all, those men on the front line needed to be patted on the back when they sold a lot of insurance and they needed to be kicked in the pants when they didn't.

As usual, Kuhns had sized up the situation accurately and had chosen the right man for the right job. Mills, as a reporter and city editor, had demonstrated his ability to write and to evaluate critically the writings of others. More important, he not only knew the techniques of good writing but also had the education, the culture, and the good taste necessary to provide substance for his writing. Having received a fine basic foundation in the liberal arts at Grinnell College, Mills continued to pursue his own liberal education throughout the rest of his life. No other company in the country could boast of an advertising manager and publications director more humanely literate than Mills, a man as conversant with the writings of Balzac, Cather, and Conrad as he was with the sales record of the field agent in Peoria, Illinois.

Very soon after Mills took office, the field force began to receive a weekly publication, *The Grit*, which soon thereafter became *The Bulletin*. As one of Mills's assistants, John Grimes, would later recall in his recollections of the company:

The Bulletin *was a 16-page little magazine in format, but it was far more newspaper than magazine in editorial philoso-*

phy. As a former newspaper man, Bert Mills believed sincerely in the old newspaper man's adage—"names make news." He wanted field names in The Bulletin *and he got them there. ... A major part of editing* The Bulletin *was the constant attempt to get from Agency Manager letters, from Regional Sales Managers, from agency bulletins, etc., the little "human interest" stories about salesmen, their families, their lives, their work.... The* Bulletin *made no pretense of being a vehicle for education or training. Its purpose more nearly paralleled that of a small town newspaper to keep people aware of other people and their doings. In retrospect it appears to have hit its mark. It did do a job in making the Bankers Life Company—in the field—a "people" company.*

Having established a line of communications between Des Moines and the field, Kuhns turned his attention to incentives. Because Bankers Life was authorized to do business in New York State, it had to abide throughout the entire nation with the very strict regulations that the New York State Insurance Commission had established after the 1906 Armstrong report. These regulations included a strict limit for each type of insurance policy on the amount of commission that could be paid the agent. A commission could be no higher in Ottumwa, Iowa, than New York would permit to be paid an agent in Manhattan. Consequently, Kuhns could not offer the promise of higher commissions as a bait for greater production. But carrots can come in many different shapes and sizes. Kuhns could offer prizes for meeting quotas, he could create clubs in which membership was limited to those who sold above a certain level, and he could provide annual outings for the star salesmen at some of the great resort centers of the nation. All of these inducements were inaugurated as soon as Kuhns was in a position of power to do so.

The first such annual convention of Bankers Life salesmen and officers was held in San Francisco in the early spring of 1915. Knowing full well the kind of exuberant, extrovertive people who always prove to be the top salesmen in any company and the boisterous way in which they can celebrate a convention, Kuhns very wisely established the policy for the first and all subsequent conventions that qualifying salesmen could bring along their wives and children at company expense. The presence of their families undoubtedly helped somewhat in holding the enthusiasm of the conventiongoers within

In 1880, Piety Hill was a famous area of Des Moines known for its many churches. The home office now stands in place of the church on the right.

Downtown Des Moines, 1888.

The first certificate of The Bankers Life Association belonged, appropriately, to its first president, Edward Temple.

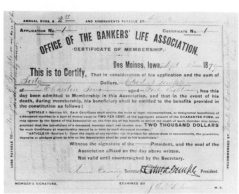

ANNUAL DUES, $ 2⁰⁰   AND ASSESSMENTS PAYABLE AT——

APPLICATION No. 1   CERTIFICATE No. 1

OFFICE OF THE BANKERS' LIFE ASSOCIATION.
CERTIFICATE OF MEMBERSHIP.

Des Moines, Iowa, Sept — 187—

This is to Certify, That in consideration of his application and the sum of ——— Dollars, —Edward Temple—

of ——Charlton, Iowa— aged——Fort-eight—, has this day been admitted to Membership in this Association, and that in the event of his death, during membership, his beneficiary shall be entitled to the benefits provided in the constitution as follows:

"ARTICLE I. Section III. Each Certificate shall entitle the holder or legal representatives, or designated beneficiary of a deceased member to a sum of money equal to TWO PER CENT. of the aggregate amount of the GUARANTEE FUND, as may appear by the books of the Association on the first day of the month in which the death of such member may occur, provided that the beneficiary of a deceased member shall not receive over TWO THOUSAND DOLLARS for each Certificate of membership issued to or held by such deceased member.

"ARTICLE III. Section I. Upon the death of any member not in arrears for annual dues or assessments, the guarantee deposits or pledges given by him to the Association shall be paid to his beneficiary.

Witness the signature of the ——— President, and the seal of the Association affixed on the day above written.

Not valid until countersigned by the Secretary.

——Simon Casady—— Secretary ——Edward Temple—— President.

MEMBER'S SIGNATURE,   EXAMINED BY ——————, M. D.

CERTIFICATE OF MEMBERSHIP

THE BANKERS LIFE ASSOC

No. 113800   Des Moines, Iowa, March

This is to Certify, That in consideration of the Arti Association and of the warranties contained in his Application No. 9454? contract and the sum of ——Forty and 50/100—— Dollars, Mr. —— of ——Lineville—— State of ——Iowa—— by occupation ——Farmer—— has been admitted to Membership in this Association and that in the event of his a receive the sum of **Two Thousand Dollars,** and the Guarantee Fund deposited w ——Twenty Seven—————— Dollars.

Upon the Failure of the above named member to make any payment due from him to the Ass October, of each year his guarantee deposit and all other payments made shall be forfeited an

This Certificate to become null and void, if death occur from self destruction within five years f member is or shall become intemperate in the use of intoxicating liquors, chloral, cocaine or be brought or sustained upon or under this certificate unless proof of death be made within the day of the death of the member. This Certificate to take effect and be in force only on de

The Amount due under this contract to be provided for by assessment on the member the Association, unless otherwise supplied, and to be paid to ——His Legal R at the Home Office of the Association upon presentation of this Certificate with satis ficiary. In the event of the death of the beneficiary prior to that of the member, or in case non representatives of the deceased member.

In Witness Whereof the signature of the President, attest are hereto affixed on the date above written.

ATTEST:

——A C Stiεssoν——
SECRETARY.

MEMBERS SIGNATURE ——Joseph E. P——

FOURTEENTH YEAR.

CALL No. 38.

OFFICE OF
THE BANKERS LIFE ASSOCIATION.

DES MOINES, IOWA, Sept. 24, 1892.

DEAR SIR:—We are pleased to inform you that *Call No. 38, due in October next, will be passed,* the Benefit Fund being in a condition so favorable that no collections need be made for that account.

This is the fourth consecutive year in which we have passed a call for payment of death losses, and in no case has the event been preceded or followed by a *double call.*

The business of the Association is steadily on the increase. It has now a round million of dollars in actual assets, has paid $900,000 in death losses, has $700,000 in State Department, and has commissioned 1900 bank depositories. It is licensed in 18 States, carries Insurance on business principles at figures which *astonish everybody,* and courts investigation upon all points.

In view of these facts you will permit the suggestion that remarks pro and con as to the Association or its management are now in order and are respectfully solicited by
Your obedient servant,

EDW'D A. TEMPLE, PRESIDENT.

Persons recommended for Membership will be supplied with circulars on receipt of address.

"Call cards" like this one were distributed to Association members when collections were made on certificates.

$2000 00

corporation and By-Laws of this which are hereby made a part of this

Perkins

aged Twenty Seven years,

membership his beneficiary shall ciation by the said member amounting to

maturity in January, April, July or hip shall thereupon cease.

the member being sane or insane, or if the his death be due thereto. No action shall and suit commenced within one year after

pro rata upon the 'Guarantee Fund of alives

of claim, to be supplied by the bene benefit then to be payable to the legal

retary, and the seal of the Association

Those people who joined The Bankers Life Association received a membership certificate like this one.

Typical office setting around 1914.

These general agents of the late 1920s were the forerunners of today's Agents' Advisory Council.

The Bankers Life Checker Club, about 1920.

The $100,000 Club was one of The Bankers Life's early clubs formed to recognize outstanding agent production. This is a portion of the group that gathered in 1914.

W-H-O

From 1925-1930 Iowans listened to the sounds of *The Bankers Life Little Symphony*, the *Apollo String Quartet*, *Myrtle Williams*, and other programs over *The Bankers Life*-owned WHO radio station.

The first advertisement for The Bankers Life Association ran in the Sunday edition of the Des Moines Leader, *July 11, 1886.*

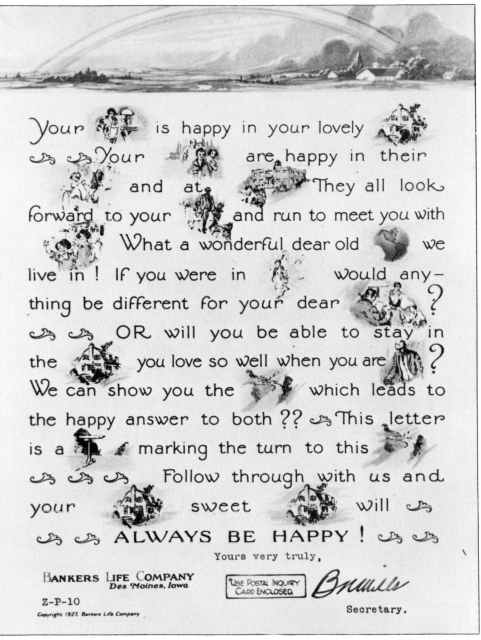

This is the first direct mail piece ever used in the life insurance industry. Introduced by The Bankers Life in 1927, the advertisement was credited with increasing new sales by nearly $3 million after its first year of use.

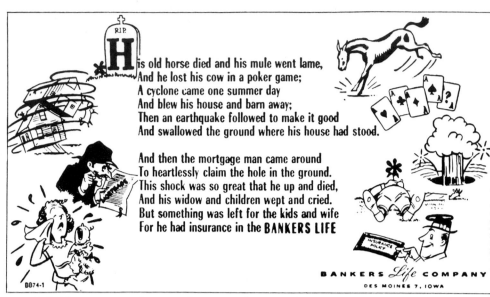

Ink blotters were favorite direct mail pieces during the 1930s and 1940s. Company records show the famous "Mule Blotter" was particularly successful in encouraging new sales.

Saturday Evening Post *readers saw this advertisement, one of the first magazine messages of The Bankers Life, in 1934.*

Double Duty Dollars became synonymous with The Bankers Life during the 1930s and 1940s.

Our free booklet will help you choose the right life insurance company.

Even if you don't choose us.

Ahh. A little peace of mind.

Selecting the right life insurance company is one of the most important decisions you'll ever make. But how do you know which one to choose? Well, you could talk with a representative from each life insurance company in the country. There are over 1800 companies.

Or you could spend a little time reading our informative booklet on how to select a life insurance company. It won't make you an expert on the subject. But it will give you enough basic knowledge so you can make a wise decision.

We promise no salesman will call. We just want to help. If you don't do business with us, we want you to pick a good competitor. Mail the coupon to The Bankers Life.

The big one that got that way by caring a little more.

The Bankers Life, Consumer Services
Des Moines, Iowa 50307
Please send me, without obligation, a free copy of "How to Select the Right Life Insurance Company."

Name_____

Address_____

City_____State_____Zip_____

THE BANKERS LIFE
BANKERS LIFE COMPANY, DES MOINES, IOWA 50307
Individual and group life, health and disability programs. Pension and profit sharing investment plans.

This 1971 advertisement, which ran in six national publications, offered consumer information booklets to people requesting copies. Additional current advertisements offer three other brochures through the home office's Consumer Services. The consumer education program began in 1968.

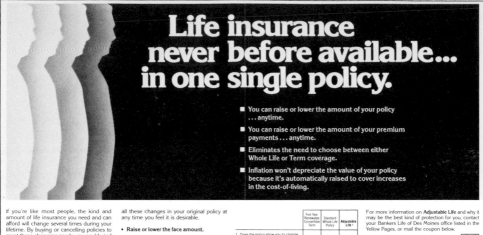

To introduce its revolutionary life insurance product, Adjustable Life, which became available to the public in 1977, The Bankers Life used advertisements like this to explain the policy's unique features.

During 1968 and 1969 Hugh Downs, nationally known TV personality, delivered the company's commercial messages every Monday morning on the TODAY Show. At a visit to the TODAY Show set (left to right) Merv Cramer, former senior vice-president, Hugh Downs, Frank Blair, and former President Earl Bucknell discussed The Bankers Life's advertising program.

THE BANKERS
LIFE ASSOCIATION

BANKERS *Life* **COMPANY**
DES MOINES

BANKERS *Life* **COMPANY**
DES MOINES, IOWA

THE BANKERS LIFE

BANKERS LIFE COMPANY   DES MOINES, IOWA

Some of the major steps in the company's history are identified by a look at the logos of The Bankers Life over the past 100 years. The present logo, adopted in 1968, graphically illustrates the concept of mutuality so important in The Bankers Life's history. A special logo was developed for use explicitly during the 1979 Centennial year.

Home offices of The Bankers Life

1879/Des Moines Bank Building

1882/211 Fourth Street

1885/Youngerman Building

1888/Iowa Loan and Trust Building

1890/Marquardt Building

1896/Equitable Building

1917/Valley National Bank Building

1924/Liberty Building

Gerard Nollen, former president of The Bankers Life, digs in at the groundbreaking of the new home office at 711 High Street, August 29, 1938.

From ground level to the highest point, the original home office building stood 145 feet, with six floors, a penthouse, and cooling tower above grade. To many people who watched the construction, it seemed impossible that such a large building would house only one company.

reasonable bounds, but even so, it is doubtful if many of them would have received a highly favorable temperance report from Mr. Temple's depository bankers of a quarter of a century before.

At these conventions, the agents received some instruction on new ideas for selling, on new policies that were being developed, on new goals that the home office hoped to reach during the coming year. The agents, in turn, would pledge their commitment to the individual goals they hoped to attain for their agencies. Above all, the conventions allowed the agents to get to know their officers and to know each other, to compare notes, and often to air their gripes. It was Kuhns's very effective way of making a community out of a large, widely dispersed, and highly individualistic sales force.

The Kuhns presidency inaugurated the golden era of the field agent—an era that was to extend down to World War II. Many insurance companies like to boast that their agents are their greatest asset, and so in truth, the agents are. But few companies did as much to make that statement meaningful to the agents themselves as did Bankers Life under George Kuhns and his successor, Gerard Nollen. The agents became the folk heroes of the Bankers Life world throughout the twenties and thirties, and the tales told and retold of the more colorful characters became the threads out of which legends are woven. One hesitates to single out a few such characters even for purposes of illustration, lest the memories of those many, many others be unfairly slighted, but surely no history of the company could fail to note C. A. "Pop" Reed, agency manager at Los Angeles, who had been born in poverty in rural Ohio, and whose one goal in life was to be wealthy enough to have a custom-designed Pierce-Arrow, painted canary yellow, with lilac-colored wheels. He finally achieved that goal, and so, dressed in a matching canary-yellow suit with a lilac pocket handkerchief, he drove his Pierce-Arrow back to Washington Court House, Ohio, to show the old hometown that the local boy had made good, only to discover that no one there remembered his name or that he had ever lived there at all. But the farmers of central South Dakota would never forget A. E. Nickelson, agency manager of that territory, who would squeeze his gigantic frame into the front seat of his Model T Ford while the back seat would be occupied by a keg of corn mash. He always told his farm customers that traveling the country roads did wonders for aging that corn liquor in just a few days. And the contents of that keg proved to be, in those Prohibition days, an excellent icebreaker in opening contacts with dusty and thirsty farmers on the South Dakota plains.

Each agent had his own highly idiosyncratic approach to potential customers. Nickelson did it with swigs of corn mash, some did it more conventionally with the calendars and desk blotters that Mills's office provided, but few had the commanding presence of Fred Thorberg of the Madison, Wisconsin, agency. Thorberg would drive into a southern Wisconsin farmyard, blare away on his horn until the farmer came running to see what was the matter, and would then give his pitch to the farmer for the Life Paid Up at 65 policy, a policy that Thorberg called "the cheese maker's special—issued only in limited amounts. There are only a few more of these policies left for this year, but sign here and I'll see if I can't get you one of those." And more times than not, the farmer would sign and Thorberg would have his sale.

Just as each salesman could develop his own individual pitch, so each agency manager was given the freedom to run his territory in his own way. Some like W. I. Fraser of the Lincoln, Nebraska, agency were martinets, who insisted upon absolute discipline and a strict adherence to rules. Fraser, whose quick temper and frequently announced resignation from the company were legendary, called monthly meetings of all of his agents to give them their orders, and if any salesman was as much as one minute late, he found the door to the manager's office locked, and he himself was left waiting outside in limbo. Others, most notably Roleigh Martin of Ottumwa, ran a very loose command indeed, believing that camaraderie produced more loyalty and more sales than did commands. Some built their agency within the confines of a metropolitan district, such as De-Forest Bowman in Chicago, and J. E. Flanigan, the former actuary of the company, in Manhattan. Others like Elbert Storer of Indianapolis managed a whole state and sent their salesmen out for a week at a time to cover the territory. Some made use of district agents, who held the top contracts with the company and served almost as surrogate agency managers. Some also made use of what was known as the "protection license procedure," which, according to John Grimes, was "another helper type situation ... [in which] the helper would be something less than a subagent. His role was usually that of a 'bird dog'—providing suspects and prospect names for the active agent to follow up. Unlike a subagent, the protection licenseman had no contract with either the agency manager or the company. On the contrary, he usually had only a verbal commitment from the agent to the effect that he would receive a stipulated rate of first-year commission on any business sold on his suspects and prospects."

The agency managers differed in personality and temperament as greatly as they did in methods of operation. There was the vain and pompous DeForest Bowman, of Chicago, who developed his own direct-mail advertising quite independent of the company and who, with his superior ways and his insistence upon complete autonomy, was a constant source of irritation to both the home office and his fellow agency managers. In contrast was the team of Jack and Dorothy Rowe, both so endearing in manner as to be favorites within the entire company. Because of their small stature, they were affectionately known as "the ponies."

There was the urbane and sophisticated G. F. Murrell of Pittsburgh, who became independently wealthy when one of his farmer customers told him one day that he was thinking of moving because his well water had developed a strange oily taste. Murrell bought the farm on the spot and with his newly acquired oil money retired to Italy. And at the opposite extreme was the former blacksmith Thorberg, who did not even know how to read or write until after his marriage, when his wife taught him.

Some agents like Martin, Flanigan, and F. W. Darling of Cedar Rapids were notoriously disrespectful of their health, eating so much and drinking so much as to cause the company's actuary, E. M. McConney, to predict that all three would die before they reached fifty. All three, however, again demonstrated their independence and also the invalidity of mass actuarial statistics as applied to specific individuals by living ten years or more beyond the time limit McConney had given them. Other agents like Bill Winterble of the Madison agency and Bob Wright of Cleveland were former star athletes, who carefully protected their health and kept their youthful physiques well into middle age.

There was, in short, no stereotype for Bankers Life salesmen and managers. They came in all shapes and sizes and from many different kinds of backgrounds. The company not only tolerated but prized eccentricity, as long as the job of selling got accomplished. The canned speech or the set sales pitch was anathema to both the home office and the individual agents. Indeed, the company, either by design or through neglect, throughout the Kuhns administration provided virtually nothing in the way of sales training. Kuhns himself believed that salesmen were born, not made, and no school or high-powered training session could produce a star "millionaire"—that is, a salesman who could sell a million dollars' worth of insurance in a year. There was an old insurance joke, frequently told throughout the industry, of the agency manager's giving instructions to his newly appointed agent. "Son, here is a Rate Book—here are some application forms and a sample policy, and now come over here to the window with me for a minute. Just look out there. Hundreds and hundreds— even thousands—of prospects. Go get 'em, Tiger!" And with that the training session was over. It is an apocryphal story, but for Bankers Life as well as for most insurance companies in the 1920s, it contained more truth than fancy.

With rate books in hand, they hit the road, the newly contracted recruit and the seasoned old veteran. It didn't take the new agent long to know that his product for Bankers Life in the 1920s, as compared with Metropolitan or Prudential, offered a rather limited range of policy plans. In the mid-twenties about 82 percent of all policies sold were of four types, Life Paid at 70, Life Paid at 65, Twenty Payment Life, and Eighteen Payment Life, with the first two kinds of policies making up over two thirds of Bankers Life's total business.

These Kuhns salesmen sold a lot of insurance: among them were W. I. Fraser, and later his son, W. A. Fraser, out in the sand hills of Nebraska, where no one was supposed to have a dollar in his pocket; as well as DeForest Bowman along the Gold Coast of the near northside in Chicago. The amount of insurance in force increased $12 million in the first year of Kuhns's presidency, nearly $50 million from 1918 to 1919, and $75 million from 1924 to 1925.

Kuhns's success with Bankers Life was earning for him a reputation for achievement throughout the insurance industry. He was one of five insurance presidents in the nation who was asked to come to Washington in early 1917, as the nation began to prepare for war, to help design the first government insurance bill for those drafted for military service. He also began to get very strong hints from other major insurance companies that they would like to consider him for a top executive position, including a direct offer of a vice-presidency with New York Life, but Kuhns had no interest. He preferred to stay where he was, the big frog in a pond that was growing ever larger.

America's entry into World War I did slow down temporarily the rate of increase, due in part to an acute shortage of salesmen, and in part to the fact that the government offered free insurance to all members of the armed forces while on active duty. But even in 1918, there was a slight increase of $9 million over that of the preceding year. It was during World War I that Bankers Life made the first philanthropic contributions in its history—$5,000 to the American

Red Cross and $1,000 to the YMCA. It did this with the encouragement and blessing of the Iowa State Insurance Commissioner, but even so, the company felt that it had to justify its giving away of its policyholders' funds in this way by stating in the Board minutes that it was giving to these two agencies "as a conservation measure for the prevention of disease and death among policyholders subject to military or naval service."

Although the company called for an extra $100 premium per annum for each $1,000 of insurance for all policyholders in military service outside the continental limits of the United States, battlefield casualties during the war presented no heavy drain on the company's reserves. Civilian casualties during the great Spanish influenza epidemic at the very end of the war, however, for which no insurance company had been able to prepare itself with added premiums, was quite another matter. The influenza epidemic of 1918–19 was the last great plague to strike the entire world's population, comparable in intensity to the Black Death of the fourteenth century and the bubonic plague of the seventeenth century. Millions of people died throughout the world, and insurance companies in the United States were badly hit. In November 1918 and again in February 1919, death claims on Bankers Life doubled and quadrupled over the actuarial probabilities, and in March 1919 Bankers Life for the first time since it had become a mutual legal reserve company was forced to suspend all dividends for a year, as did many other companies. By the summer of 1919, however, the disease had vanished as mysteriously as it had appeared. The death rate dropped to the normal expectancy, and insurance sales soared. Both the war and the epidemic had proven to be great stimulants to the public's demand for life insurance.

In order to secure as much of this expanding market as possible, Kuhns accelerated the company's advertising campaigns. His advertising manager, Bert Mills, pioneered within the insurance industry in direct-mail advertising. Agents were told to submit names of any possible prospects—no matter how remotely possible they might be—within the agents' territories. The company would then, at no expense to the agent, mail out a personally addressed letter to that prospect pointing up the wisdom of buying life insurance and informing the potential customer that he would soon be called upon by the company's representative who could explain in greater detail the various kinds of policies and forms of protection the company offered. There was no selectivity involved on the part of the agent submitting the names. Indeed, Merwyn Cramer, who was then as a young man selling insurance for the W. I. Fraser agency, obtained his list of names in each small town within his territory by simply copying the names in the local telephone directory. The letters went out by the thousands. The agent could then go into the field and approach a prospect with the opening line, "Mr. Smith, I believe you got a letter from my company just last week, and they have asked me to call on you to see if you have any questions." It was a simple but quite novel idea. And it worked. Other companies very quickly adopted the technique.

With a rapidly expanding business in the immediate post-World War I years, it was soon apparent that the home office was rapidly outgrowing the space provided for it in the Valley National Bank Building into which the company had only recently moved in 1917 from the old Equitable Building. And it was in providing new office space for the home office that E. W. Nothstine was to perform his last service for the Bankers Life Company.

By 1920 George Kuhns had come reluctantly to the conclusion that his old friend no longer had a future with the company. Nothstine's personal financial affairs were in constant disarray and there was a growing suspicion and fear among his colleagues that his personal finances might also involve company finances. Nothstine borrowed heavily from Kuhns and from anyone else in the company gullible enough to be taken in. It was also evident to Kuhns that in Bill Jaeger he had a man who was as good a salesman as Nothstine had ever been and, in addition, commanded the loyalty and respect of both the home office and the field. Nothstine had been quite correct in viewing Jaeger as a potential threat to his own position in the company. Once the painful decision was made, Kuhns with characteristic vigor was prepared to act. Jaeger would come into the home office as general sales manager to replace Nothstine. But also with characteristic loyalty to an old friend, Kuhns was prepared to give Nothstine one last chance to redeem himself with his associates and incidentally to promote a venture that should greatly improve his own personal fortunes.

On January 19, 1922, the Board authorized Kuhns to send Nothstine a letter in which the company agreed to lease at two dollars per square foot sufficient space in a new office building to be erected on the southwest corner of Sixth and Grand Avenue. On May 17, the Board signed a lease for the top five floors of this proposed new building and paid for a year's rent in advance. With this money in his pocket and this backing from Bankers Life, Nothstine was able to secure the necessary funding to construct the Liberty Building, which would be Bankers Life's home office quarters for the next fifteen years. Having obtained this final boon from his patron, Nothstine, as per agreement, resigned as general sales manager on July 1, 1922, and Jaeger was immediately appointed to succeed him.

The Liberty Building may have set Nothstine at liberty from Bankers Life, but it did not free him from future financial and personal difficulties. Happily for the management of the Liberty Building and also for its major tenant, Nothstine's interest in the new office building he had promoted proved to be as evanescent as all of his other will-o'-the-wisp dreams for quick wealth. Shortly after leaving Bankers Life and long before the Liberty Building was completed, Nothstine ran off with the wife of one of the company's St. Louis agents. When last heard of by his former Bankers Life associates, he was busily promoting stock in a company that proposed to manufacture a perpetual-motion machine. If only Nothstine's ingenuity for fraudulent schemes could have been harnessed, there indeed might have been a machine whose motion was perpetual.

Having acquired a lease of five floors in Des Moines' newest and most spacious office building, Kuhns had at last room for expansion, and he had some very expansive ideas. Late in 1924, just after moving into the Liberty Building, Kuhns decided to buy a radio station. Perhaps no other advertising idea that Kuhns's busy imagination conceived of had as great an impact upon the general public as this. There was for sale in Des Moines a small Class B commercial station of 500-watt power with a range limited to 150 miles. It had begun operations on April 10, 1924, and its owners, who had already secured the necessary equipment to increase its power to 5,000 watts, were now prepared to sell it to Kuhns for $60,000. The idea was immediately appealing to Kuhns for a variety of reasons. First, he saw it as a major advertising vehicle for his company; second, with his genuine interest in agriculture, he could envision this station's becoming a major force in promoting the interests of the Midwest farmers; and third, for a very personal compelling argument, he wanted the station because he saw at last an opportunity to place his recently acquired son-in-law, W. H. Heinz, who had a mechanical engineering degree from the University of Pittsburgh, in a responsible position within the company. The other Board directors, who lacked Kuhns's vision and his personal family obligations, were less than enthusiastic over the proposal, but as usual, Kuhns prevailed. In March 1925 the Board reluctantly authorized him to purchase the station at a cost not to exceed $57,000, "with the understanding that if said station is purchased the circularizing furnished by the company for the agents will be reduced to one-half the amount now provided."

If the agents had been allowed a vote, they undoubtedly would have voted heavily in favor of continuing the "circularizing" at full amount rather than investing heavily in what many must have regarded as some kind of crazy gimcrack toy. But Kuhns was far more imaginative and advanced in his thinking than were his conservative Board or his agents. Radio in 1925 was still a toy, much as citizen band transmitters and receivers were in the early 1970s, but Kuhns could see its great potential as a salesman which would soon have easy entry into almost every living room in America.

Bankers Life was not getting much in the way of equipment or power for its $57,000, but quite by happenstance, due to a lucky allocation by the Commerce Department, this small station in Iowa had been given a clear channel near the top of the dial at 570 kilocycles. This particular assignment gave the station a range far beyond that which might be expected of a 5,000-watt station. Furthermore, the call letters assigned the station, WHO, were an advertiser's dream. The 1920s was the age of the advertising slogan when a catchy phrase, such as "I'd Walk a Mile for a Camel," or "Ask the Man Who Owns One," was far more important in selling a product than was the quality of the goods being sold. It took no great inspiration upon Bert Mills's part to come up with the perfect station identification slogan: "This is WHO—WHO?—Bankers Life, Des Moines, Iowa." WHO quickly became the most famous call letters throughout the Midwest, and Bankers Life was securely tied to that fame.

Bankers Life had hardly settled into its new quarters on the top five floors of the Liberty Building than the building was sprouting two strange insectlike feelers—two towers on the roof which supported the station's antenna. The radio studio, announcer's booth, and mechanical area were located on the top floor of the building. The office of the station's general manager, Kuhns's son-in-law, Bill Heinz, was on the east side of the floor, directly off the elevator lobby. Heinz had the title and the prestige, but the real power of control over programming and advertising lay in Bert Mills's office two floors down.

In these early days of radio, the actual programs presented were not nearly as important as the fact that they were being presented. Radio was rather like Mark Twain's talking dog. It didn't matter much what it said—what was impressive was that it talked at all. Those thousands of persons who had radio receivers by 1925 were primarily interested in "logging," that is, in turning the dial at different hours of the day or night to see what stations they could pick up. The call letters of the station received would be duly noted on the log along with the time of receipt, and men at work the next day would casually mention, "Picked up WGN Chicago last night. Came in clear as a bell."

Sometimes listeners would write a card of appreciation to the station that they had heard just as people will answer a note received in a bottle from the sea, and Bankers Life began to hear from people throughout the Midwest—International Falls, Minnesota; Terre Haute, Indiana; Salina, Kansas; and once even, due to some atmospheric quirk, from Winnipeg, Canada. Kuhns and Mills saw a potential market gold mine in this popular indoor sport, so they prepared a radio map of the United States showing the location of all existing radio stations along with a neatly printed log with columns for stations heard, date, and time. These log maps were sent out by the thousands along with a brief notation, "WHO is the biggest insurance company in the Midwest? WHO? Bankers Life, of course. See our agent for your insurance needs."

Logging may have been the public's major interest in radio, but Kuhns and Mills hoped to be able to provide the kind of programming that would not only attract the listener to the top of the dial but once there, he or she would stay and listen. Bankers Life was exceedingly fortunate in finding locally a young man, Dean Cole, whose mellifluous voice quickly made him the favorite radio announcer in the entire region. Old King Cole, as he called himself, proved to be one of the greatest pitchmen in the history of radio. And in addition to his Fiddlers Three, King Cole offered a great variety of local musical talent. The business manager of Drake University, Fred Turby, was as publicity-minded as George Kuhns himself, and consequently, it was not difficult to get a lot of free musical talent from the university's excellent School of Music, which was then under the direction of Arcule Sheasby.

Bankers Life people themselves had talent to offer. Bert Mills's wife, Lora Ladd Mills, had received excellent training prior to the war in Boston and Berlin for her very fine soprano voice, and she made frequent "guest star" appearances on WHO. Two of the home office staff, George Carpenter and Ed Wright, formed a dance band which played for WHO, and several employees, including Claire Marshall and O. B. Jackman's grandson, Jack Jackman, sang in barbershop quartets for the station. Jack Scovel, supervisor of the Policy Loan Division, did an occasional stint as relief announcer for Dean Cole, and young John Grimes, in Mills's office, broadcast three Drake football games for WHO during his first year at Bankers Life. Time was always available for George Kuhns or Gerard Nollen to speak to the public on the serious matter of insurance. The station, in short, was quite a family affair for the company, the university, and the city of Des Moines. A typical day of programming in the mid-1920s might be as follows:

> 7:00–8:00 A.M. Setting-up exercises.
>
> 8:00–9:00 A.M. Off the air (presumably to recover from the calisthentics).
>
> 9:00–10:30 A.M. Full government reports. (There was not much government to report on in these halcyon Cal Coolidge days, so it is difficult to imagine how this amount of time could be used each day in this area, but presumably a great deal of attention was given to Department of Agriculture reports.)
>
> 10:30–11:30 A.M. Off the air (again, presumably to recover from the government reports).
>
> 11:30 A.M.–12:30 P.M. Full government reports again. (What on earth, or rather, what on the air were they talking about?)
>
> 12:30–2:00 P.M. Off the air (lunch and siesta time).
>
> 2:00–4:00 P.M. Afternoon concert and close of market reports.
>
> 4:00–7:30 P.M. Off the air.
>
> 7:30–9:00 P.M. Evening concerts.
>
> 9:00–11:00 P.M. Off the air.
>
> 11:00–12:00 P.M. Midnight Nighthawks (for those persistent insomniacs who had not gone to bed between nine and eleven).

It is interesting to note that there was no regularly scheduled time for news broadcasts, sports, or weather unless these items were slipped in among the "full government reports."

George Kuhns had been quite sincere in his expressed desire to take over WHO in order to aid the midwestern farmer. He truly wanted to make WHO "the Voice of the Middle West," and by Middle West he meant the farmer. This empathy for the farmer on his part was not, of course, totally altruistic. The farmer had always been a major customer for Bankers Life insurance policies. Much of the company's money was invested in farm mortgage loans. The health of the company was very directly related to the financial well-being of the farmer, and the farmer in the mid-twenties was not a very active participant in the so-called Coolidge prosperity. The farmer had known hard times ever since 1921 when the World War I agrarian bubble of inflated land, grain, and livestock prices had burst.

Kuhns made his radio station available to agricultural experts, to farm leaders, to extension workers and to anyone else who had some idea as to how the plight of the family farmer could be alleviated. One of several ideas that were advanced at this time which particularly caught Kuhns's fancy was the proposal to make table sugar out of the glucose in corn. Here was a potentially new source of wealth that every Iowa and Illinois farmer had in great abundance. WHO quickly became as much of a huckster for corn sugar as it was for insurance. There was a Corn Sugar Orchestra, consisting of some Grinnell College students, who played on the air daily throughout the summer of 1925. In addition the station offered free samples of corn sugar for home testing to anyone who wrote in requesting a package. For years afterward, in the basement of the Liberty Building, there were stored hundreds of George Kuhns's packets of corn sugar, for unfortunately for him and the Iowa farmer there were few orders to purchase corn sugar after the initial free sample.

As the year 1925 drew to a close, in spite of the discontent among his farmer friends and his failure to sell the nation on corn sugar, George Kuhns had reason to feel satisfied with his ten-year tenure as president and to look forward with confidence to the future. He had assumed power over a company stricken with the crisis of conversion and had built it into the largest mutual legal reserve insurance company west of the Mississippi. He had seen the amount of insurance in force double and the assets more than quadruple (from $19.5 million to $81 million). Kuhns fully expected that before the decade was out, before the company would celebrate its fiftieth anniversary in 1929, Bankers Life would pass the $1 billion mark in insurance in force. And he fully expected to be there as president to celebrate that event, for at the age of sixty-four, George Kuhns was in the vigorous good health of a man who had not known a sick day in his entire busy life.

Neither of his sanguine expectations was to be fulfilled. One morning, early in December 1925, while meticulously grooming himself, as he always did, for his days' activities, he plucked a hair from his nostril—a trivial act, one that he had performed a thousand times. But this time infection set in. Within a week, septicemia had spread throughout his body. He battled for his life for six weeks, but in those pre-antibiotic days there were no wonder drugs to come to his assistance. On January 12, 1926, when Kuhns's death appeared near, the Board of Directors quickly passed a resolution granting "the President, Mr. Kuhns, ... a leave of absence until July 1, 1926, and in view of his ill health that the allowance of salary be paid to him forthwith in advance." On the following morning, George Kuhns died. A man who had never before been stopped by any combination of men or circumstances was now felled by a wound more minuscule even than the small prick of the arrow that had barely punctured Achilles' heel. On the day of Kuhns's funeral, Governor John Hammill ordered all state flags flown at half mast in his honor. George Kuhns's widow had reason to be grateful for the Board's timely generosity in granting him a half year's salary in advance, one day before his death. When his affairs were settled, it was discovered that other than his life insurance he had left his family little in the way of an estate. He had apparently paid dearly for his friendship with Nothstine in loans that had never been repaid, in real estate ventures in Minnesota and Kansas that had failed, even in perpetual motion machines that had never moved. But to Bankers Life, he left a far richer legacy in staff personnel whom he had hired, in policies and programs he had inaugurated, in a spirit he had inspired, and this estate continued to pay dividends for the next fifty years.

Bankers Life was holding its annual meeting of the President's Gold Medal Club in Monterey, California, when the word was received that George Kuhns was dead. The meeting was immediately adjourned, and the top officers in attendance hurried back to Des Moines for the funeral and for the inauguration of a new order. Incredible as it might seem, the king nevertheless was dead, and the succession had to be attended to.

Simon Casady, the only surviving founding father of Bankers Life, had long nurtured the hope that the presidency might be his. He had regarded himself as the heir apparent to Temple only to see the prize go to Clark. He surely must have known after 1912 that he had no chance of blocking Kuhns's ascension to the throne, but now he had survived even Kuhns. Surely this time, he felt, he could not be denied. He was old and tired and would not want the office long, just long enough to have the pleasure of savoring the honor that was due him. In these vain dreams, he was aided and abetted by Clinton Nourse.

The death of George Kuhns, however, had come as a traumatic shock to the entire company. This was no time to indulge in historic sentiment. Although Kuhns had never discussed retirement or prepared anyone to be his successor, it seemed quite evident to most of the Board that the only logical choice was the vice-president, Gerard Nollen.

The Board met on January 19, two days after Kuhns's funeral, to take up the question of the presidency. Nourse immediately moved, seconded by Casady, that "the election of a Director to fill the vacancy caused by the death of Mr. Kuhns be deferred until the annual meeting in April." It was clearly a trial balloon on Nourse's and Casady's parts. Had the Board accepted this motion, Nourse was prepared to move that the election of a president also be deferred until April in the hope that during the intervening time sentiment could be further fostered for Casady's election. Gerard Nollen was shrewd enough certainly to see what Nourse was up to. Nollen was usually a quiet, unemotional man, but he was also a determined Dutchman. Those who were present at the Board meeting were privileged to hear Nollen speak out with an angry vigor that they had never heard before and were never to hear again. He proceeded to tell the Board in no uncertain terms that it had a business to manage, that no matter how shocking Kuhns's death was to all of them, the Board could not indulge itself in a three-month mourning period of inactivity. Board vacancies and presidential chairs had to be filled now. Business had to go on as before or surely it would cease altogether.

As soon as Nollen finished speaking the Nourse motion was defeated, 4 to 2, and Dr. Ross Huston, the medical director, was then elected to fill Kuhns's place on the Board, with Casady and Nourse dissenting. Accepting the inevitable, Nourse then moved that Gerard Nollen be elected president. It was only a halfhearted gesture toward reconciliation, however, for Nourse added a clause to his motion, stipulating that Nollen's salary was "to remain the same as he has heretofore been receiving as Vice President." The motion passed unanimously. G. W. Fowler, the company's secretary, was then elected vice-president to replace Nollen, and W. W. Jaeger was appointed as a second vice-president and director of agencies. O. B. Jackman, who had earlier been brought in from the field where he had served as regional sales manager to be Jaeger's assistant, now moved up the ladder along with his much younger boss to become assistant director of agencies.

So Bankers Life got a Nollen at the head of the firm after all. This time the effort at Nollen blocking had failed, which is not surprising. Casady and Nourse combined had hardly proved to be the equal of a Kuhns acting alone. But then for that matter, Gerard was a somewhat more sophisticated Nollen than his brother had been. A new team had been formed, and Bankers Life was in business as usual.

4/Years of Trials and Triumphs

1926-1938

With the election of Gerard S. Nollen as the fourth president of Bankers Life on January 19, 1926, the company was reestablishing a particular presidential model that had been set by Temple but had been abandoned with the selection of George Kuhns as president. This is not to imply, of course, that each of the nine presidents that the company has had during its first one hundred years of existence has not been a distinct personality, with his own individual strengths and weaknesses, his own mode of operations and style. But companies tend to create their own corporate images which are reflected in their choice of chief executives, and Nollen was admirably true to the Bankers Life image. Like Temple, Clark, and the men who were to succeed him, but unlike Kuhns, Nollen was basically conservative and moderate in behavior, manner, and philosophy. Kuhns was an autocrat, whose will was never thwarted; the others have been essentially company men, who have preferred to achieve a consensus rather than to rule by decree.

Nollen was to establish a new pattern for the presidency which would hold for his five successors. He had joined Bankers Life in 1912 as an actuary, and all of those who were to succeed him have also come out of the actuarial department. An actuary by temperament is of a different breed from that of a field agent. The presidential office lost something in the way of flamboyance, color, and aggressiveness when it did not continue in the Kuhns format, but this loss was compensated in part by the gaining of extramural respectability and intraoffice harmony. Edmund McConney, one of Nollen's successors,

67

had called Kuhns "the right man for the right time in the company's history." But so also was Nollen right for his time. The company was fortunate in getting each man as president for the particular time in which he served.

Nollen was an aristocrat, scion of the Scholte and Nollen families of Pella, who were people of wealth, culture, and a high degree of intelligence. John and Johanna Scholte Nollen had had five children, three sons and two daughters. In the 1930s the three sons were each presidents of major institutions in Iowa, Henry of Equitable Life of Iowa, Gerard of Bankers Life, and the middle son, John, was president of Grinnell College. The two daughters, Sara and Hanna, founded and ran one of Des Moines' best private elementary schools. It would be impossible to find a comparable record of achievement within a single generation for any other family in Iowa.

Gerard Nollen brought to the presidency a keen, shrewdly analytical mind, a receptivity for new ideas, and a tolerance for differing points of view. By nature reserved, perhaps even somewhat shy, he was nevertheless an effective speaker. Although he lacked Kuhns's aggressive drive, he could be forceful and was not afraid to make hard decisions. If the field agents would never regard him as they had Kuhns as one of their own, if they could never imagine him calling on a prospect to make the hard sale, they nevertheless did hold him in great respect, and they very quickly realized that their interests would be as well protected by him as they had been under Kuhns. The agents found particular comfort in the fact that Bill Jaeger, who was clearly of them and for them, had a dominant voice in the Nollen administration. In many respects, Jaeger was the Kuhns surrogate during the Nollen years, able to provide precisely those qualities of personality and that interest in and love for selling that Kuhns had had and that Nollen lacked. The team of Nollen and Jaeger was an effective combination.

Kuhns may have left the company a rich legacy, but he also left Nollen with some difficult problems. The most immediate and pressing problem was that of the $200 million worth of assessment certificates still outstanding—nearly one quarter of the total amount of insurance in force with Bankers Life. After the second campaign in 1915–16 to get the assessment members to convert their certificates into life insurance policies, with only modestly successful results, Kuhns had largely ignored the assessment members. Regular quarterly assessment calls had been made at the normal 15 percent of the certificate holders' original guarantee deposit. But high mortality rates during the influenza epidemic had forced the company to dip into the emergency reserve fund for the first time. As long as that fund existed, however, the quarterly calls remained the same and the old assessment members were still getting life insurance at but a fraction of the premium cost for straight life insurance policies. It is not surprising that a great many held on to their certificates and refused to convert.

By the time of Kuhns's death, however, the emergency reserve fund was all but depleted. With those remaining certificate holders growing older each year and thus subject to a higher mortality rate, with no new members coming in and no reserve fund to supplement the low rate of assessment calls, within a year the assessment calls would of necessity have to be increased drastically. This could only engender great ill will for the company. Nollen decided that the issue could no longer be ignored.

In December 1926 Nollen therefore inaugurated a final all-out effort for conversion which he called the Good Will Campaign. The campaign was to run from January 1 through March 31, 1927, but as it did not actually get under way until late in January, the time period was extended through the month of April. Nollen and Jaeger decided to use their own sales force for this campaign rather than to employ one of several outside agencies then in existence which specialized in policy conversion for the many assessment companies that had reorganized as mutual or corporate insurance companies. Nollen and Jaeger made this decision for two reasons: (1) they wanted their own salesmen rather than outside experts to get the commission, and (2) they felt their own agents would be more effective in persuading certificate holders to change or at least to bear no great ill will against the company. In many respects, it was a costly decision, for agents were to give top priority to conversion at the expense of soliciting new business. This three-and-a-half-month hiatus undoubtedly lost the company some very good prospects and broke the stride of agents in their pursuit of new business.

But Nollen was determined that, if at all possible, every one of the some eighty thousand certificate holders would be called upon personally and be given the opportunity to convert and to know in advance what it would cost them in terms of assessment rates if they did not convert. The agents were to be well paid for this endeavor—a salary of thirty-five dollars a week while engaged in the campaign; commissions comparable to those on first-year new policies (with the appropriate production credit for eligibility in the Premier Club); and finally one dollar for every card that the agent could get signed by a certificate holder to prove that the call had been made, whether or not the holder actually converted. The salesmen were told this campaign would be final as far as conversion was concerned. After April 30, all certificate holders who might wish belatedly to convert would have to deal directly with the home office, not through the agents in their area, and there would never again be any commission paid to an agent for a certificate conversion.

It was an all-out last-ditch effort. Nearly every certificate holder was called upon, but not all were persuaded by any means. Nor could it be argued that more goodwill was engendered than ill will. Of the 107,000 certificates in force at the beginning of the campaign, 31,500 were converted, but 37,000 were simply allowed to lapse when their holders were informed that the call for the first quarter of the next year might be 50 percent of the guarantee fund instead of the usual 15 percent. Nearly 40,000 certificates, however, were kept in force. Most of these owners simply refused to believe that the assessment rates would be raised. Some felt that if the rates should be raised they would have recourse in the law. So the great Good Will Campaign ended with nearly $100 million worth of certificates still in force. It had probably been worth the effort and the cost, however, for it meant the company had increased its legal reserve insurance in force by $63 million, and above all, it did strengthen Bankers Life's position when the inevitable lawsuits followed.

On March 1, 1927, in the midst of the Good Will Campaign, the Board passed Assessment Call #176 for 45 percent of the original guarantee deposit for the death benefit fund. This compared with the previous Assessment Call #175 passed on December 6, 1926, when the levy had been 13 percent. This increase offered clear evidence of what was going to happen to assessment rates now that the emergency reserve fund was depleted and undoubtedly helped to encourage many conversions. But it also promptly brought about legal action. Several disgruntled and obdurate certificate holders started suits against Bankers Life. These several suits were all consolidated as a class action suit on behalf of all the assessment holders by order of the trial court into a single suit, that of Joseph Wall et al., Plaintiffs, vs. Bankers Life Company of Des Moines, Defendant. Joseph Wall of Carroll, Iowa (no relation, it should be parenthetically and hastily added, to the author of this history), had purchased a certificate in The Bankers Life Association at the age of thirty-four on June 30, 1892. He now brought suit against the Bankers Life Company on March 9,

1927, and was represented in court by Attorneys Salinger of Carroll and Bump of Des Moines. In addition to its own chief counsel, W. S. Ayres, the son of Judge O. B. Ayres, who had succeeded to that position upon the death of Earle in 1919, Bankers Life employed an outside legal firm, Bradshaw, Shenk, and Fowler.

The major arguments of the plaintiffs were: (1) the company had improperly used the assessment members' contingent fund to help pay the expenses for conversion in 1911, and (2) the company had adequate reserves from its legal reserve funds to pay the death benefits of the Association certificate holders without raising the assessment calls above the limits originally contracted for when the certificates had been sold. In a sense, these two major arguments were contradictory, for in the first instance the plaintiffs were arguing that their funds should have been kept entirely separate and that they were not responsible for the general expenses of the company, while in the second instance they were arguing that the reserve funds of the regular insurance policyholders should be used to pay for their death benefits over and above what they had paid in to the company.

The case was of critical importance to the company for if Wall et al. should win, it would mean that assessment calls could not be raised and the excess costs would have to be borne by the legal reserve policyholders in the form of increased premiums. Quite obviously, in that case, Bankers Life would no longer be in a competitive position with other mutual legal reserve companies and could be forced out of business. In reality, the plaintiffs had no case at all, however. The agreement that assessment calls would not exceed a certain fixed limit had always been contingent upon the existence of an emergency reserve fund. If that fund should ever be depleted, as it was by 1927, the Association clearly had the right to raise assessment calls to a level adequate to cover the death benefits. That right was basic to the assessment plan concept.

The district court in the summer of 1927 found for Bankers Life on every legal point raised by the plaintiffs. The case was then appealed to the Iowa Supreme Court, which on January 23, 1929, affirmed the decision of the district court. The Iowa Supreme Court in its opinion cited the opinion of the Massachusetts Supreme Court in a similar case of *Delaney* versus *Grand Lodge A.O.U.W.*, 138 N.E. 918:

> *These members have had the benefit of insurance for them-*
> *selves and their families for many years, at very much less*

*than the cost of their insurance to the corporation. They have
had the good fortune to survive, and therefore their contracts
have brought them no money, but all the time they have had
the stipulated security against the risk of death. If now they
are called upon to pay for future insurance no more than its
cost to the corporation, they ought not to think it unjust.*

But Wall et al. did think it unjust, and they appealed to the United
States Supreme Court, an appeal that Bankers Life in no way discouraged, for it wished to get the matter settled, once and for all. In
1931 the case appeared on the U. S. Supreme Court docket. McConney, who had been appointed actuary of the company in 1924 and who
had prepared most of the financial exhibits for the case, would later
recall the scene in the old Supreme Court room in the United States
Capitol building. As soon as Attorney Salinger had launched into his
arguments for the appellants, Chief Justice Charles E. Hughes
abruptly interrupted. "Mr. Salinger, have you ever heard of the case of
Polk versus Mutual Reserve?" This was a case, celebrated among
insurance companies, in which the U. S. Supreme Court had found
for the Mutual Reserve Association against some of its assessment
members at the time it had converted into a mutual legal reserve
company. The embarrassed Salinger, who had been stopped in mid-
sentence, managed to sputter out a weak "Yes, Your Honor, I believe I
have." "Well," Chief Justice Hughes pronounced, "this is exactly the
same case, and the Court does not wish to hear you further." The Wall
case was finally over.

In the next decade, thousands of certificate holders allowed
their certificates to lapse as the Depression and the ever-rising
assessment calls, which reached a peak of 200 percent in 1949, made
it impossible for many of the old assessment members to meet the
demands. But a few tenaciously clung on to their certificates. In 1952
for the few score certificates still in force, the company decided that
no further calls would be necessary. The holders had through sheer
persistence and longevity earned the right to hold on to their
membership in Mr. Temple's Association. The last assessment member, Walter A. Teipel of Milwaukee, Wisconsin, passed away December 1978, at the age of ninety-one. Teipel, who had purchased his
$2,000 certificate of membership in 1909 at the age of twenty-two,
held the last certificate of membership in an association that ceased
operations sixty-seven years before.

Another Kuhns legacy that soon was to force Nollen to make a hard decision was that of the radio station WHO. The station had been a money loser from the beginning, in spite of its great popularity with listeners throughout the Midwest. In a letter to Major General Charles Saltzman, chairman of the Federal Radio Commission, in April 1929, Nollen stated that the average cost of the station to Bankers Life was $50,000 per year. This loss was due mainly to the fact that Bankers Life had never made an aggressive effort to sell radio time to outside advertisers. Rather it had preferred to use the station almost exclusively as an advertising vehicle for its own insurance. Therefore this cost simply had to be considered as a part of Bankers Life's advertising budget. Kuhns had so viewed it, and Nollen had accepted that point of view.

Since Kuhns's death, however, radio had quickly grown into a major business as millions of radio sets were sold throughout the nation and new radio stations by the hundreds were coming into operation. National network chains were also being established, providing local stations with programs sponsored by national advertisers. Bankers Life could no longer expect to keep its preferred clear channel at the top of the dial in order to peddle its own wares.

On September 4, 1927, WHO became an affiliate of the NBC network, and within two years was receiving twenty-six hours of programming each week from NBC, including such national favorites as *The Chase and Sanborn Hour*, *The Maxwell House Coffee Hour*, *Seth Parker*, the *Clicquot Club Eskimos* and *The National Farm and Home Hour*. Of these twenty-six hours provided by NBC, the network paid WHO for fourteen hours and forty-five minutes of the time, but for the remaining eleven hours and fifteen minutes, Bankers Life had to foot the bill. WHO continued to provide a great many local programs for its audience. With the development of small mobile transmitting units, WHO could now take its listeners "directly to the Palm Room of the Hotel Fort Des Moines" to hear the Paul Christiansen band. Its own studio was still open to company and local Des Moines talent. But increasingly, a more sophisticated listening audience preferred to hear national celebrities. Paul Christiansen in the Palm Room could not compete with Paul Whiteman at the Astor Hotel, the Bankers Life Trio was no match for the Clicquot Club Eskimos, and the public now wanted Amos and Andy, not the Maytag Radioettes. Clearly, if Bankers Life intended to remain in the radio field, it was going to have to build a staff, in both the technical and the advertising areas, to increase its facilities and to become aggressive in selling advertising.

The issue came to a head early in 1928 when abruptly WHO was informed that it would be issued a new operating license to operate on a frequency of 1,000 kilocycles. This was no longer a clear channel. WHO would hereafter have to share time with WOC, a Davenport station owned and operated by the B. J. Palmer School of Chiropractic. WHO and WOC both put in a formal protest, and WHO asked its listeners to write to the station or directly to the Federal Radio Commission if they opposed this change. The response was gratifying. The letters and telegrams poured in by the thousands forcing the commission to reopen the question and to hold public hearings.

With this kind of public support, Bankers Life fully expected to win its battle with the federal bureaucracy. On the evening before the company's assistant legal counsel, Joe Lorentzen, was to depart for Washington, carrying with him a trunkload of letters and petitions to present to the commission, the Greater Des Moines Committee held a send-off dinner for him which in effect was a victory celebration. But when Lorentzen joined Bill Heinz, the station manager, in Washington, he quickly discovered that the commission was unimpressed by the demonstrated affection of the rural Midwest for WHO. Radio was not the same kind of communications medium as the printing press. There were only a limited number of channels available for the entire nation, and an insurance company and a chiropractic school in Iowa could no longer hope to keep their own clear channels. On November 10, 1928, WHO received a blunt, final answer by telegram: "License has been issued authorizing you to operate on frequency one thousand KCs using five thousand watts power effective November eleventh at three a.m. Eastern standard time stop your station share with WOC."

Reluctantly WHO and WOC were forced into a marriage that neither wanted. One week WHO would have the right to broadcast during the daylight hours and WOC would get the evening hours. The following week they would exchange times. But it was a mismatch from the beginning. WOC was a 50,000-watt station. During the hours it was on, it could be heard throughout the Midwest. But WHO, with only 5,000 watts power and no longer having its excellent position for reception at the top of the dial, could not be heard very clearly for more than a hundred-mile radius from Des Moines.

Nollen made one final effort to get the commission to change its decision. In April 1929, in his letter to Saltzman mentioned above, Nollen pleaded for a reconsideration. He concluded with a personal note that he had been delighted to see in a recent alumni magazine that Saltzman, like Nollen, was a graduate of Grinnell College. But even this appeal to the old school tie was to no avail. The commission's decision stood.

Bankers Life now had the option of going into radio in a much larger way than ever before by investing heavily in equipment that would increase its power to 50,000 watts and in beating the bushes for local and national advertisers or of getting out altogether. Sentiment within the home office was strong for the second alternative. Kuhns had forced the station on the company in the first instance. The agents in the field had never been as enthusiastic over this form of advertising as they were for direct-mail advertising, whose budget had suffered. And some of the younger officers of the company were much opposed to continuing the station. McConney, to whose advice Nollen was increasingly receptive, was particularly strong in opposition. He warned of the increasing costs and he threw in as an added scare argument that the company and ultimately its policyholders would be held responsible in any successful suit for any libelous material that might be broadcast. This financial responsibility, McConney warned, would not be tolerated by the Iowa insurance commissioner.

These arguments were persuasive for Nollen. Negotiations for sale were begun in the summer of 1929, and in February 1930, WHO was sold to the Palmer WOC interests for $162,000, which proved to be one of the best bargains that the Davenport manipulator of low vertebrae and high finance ever got. Bankers Life hereafter would concern itself with selling insurance and not radio airtime. For years afterward, however, listeners throughout the Midwest, when they heard the familiar call letters WHO, continued, subliminally at least, to fill in the rest of the old slogan, "WHO? Bankers Life, Des Moines, Iowa." Kuhns's foray into the realm of modern communications had certainly not been a total loss to the company.

With his attempted liquidation of the assessment certificates and his successful liquidation of the radio station, Nollen clearly showed within the first three years of his presidency that a new, strong hand was at the controls. Yet, in many respects, there was little disruption in the methods of operations or of policies that had been established by Kuhns. So smooth had the transition been that field agents visiting the home office in the late twenties could find little change from what they had known in the Kuhns years. There were, to be sure, a few new stars in the ascendancy and a few former luminaries who were disappearing from the scene. The actuaries were becoming more prominent in the Nollen administration: Edmund McConney and his brilliant young assistant, Dennis Warters, gave clear indication as to which area the center of power was slowly shifting. G. W. Fowler, the former secretary of the company, became vice-president and treasurer when the last of the founding fathers, Simon Casady, died in 1929. And to succeed Fowler, Bert Mills became secretary while still retaining his position as director of advertising and publications. When William Ayres died in the same year, he was replaced by R. B. Alberson as general counsel.

With Jaeger as vice-president and director of agencies, second only to Nollen in power, the visiting field agent would feel quite at home, however, for Bankers Life, as it had been under Kuhns, remained a sales-oriented company. Most of Kuhns's promotional and communications policies were kept intact. Much of the advertising material put out in these years would by today's standards appear to be crude and unsophisticated. The message was quite clearly pitched toward a rural audience. One of the most popular bits of advertising that Mills's office ever produced was a blotter containing the following piece of doggerel (authorship unknown):

> His old horse died and his mule went lame,
> And he lost his cow in a poker game;
> A cyclone came one summer day
> And blew his house and barn away;
> Then an earthquake followed to make it good
> And swallowed the ground where his house had stood.
>
> And then the mortgage man came around
> To heartlessly claim the hole in the ground.
> This shock was so great that he up and died,
> And his widow and children wept and cried.
> But something was left for the kids and wife
> For he had insurance in the BANKERS LIFE.

These blotters were distributed by the thousands all over the nation and for many years Bankers Life was familiarly known as the Mule Blotter Company.

Although women had obtained the vote in 1920, the country was still a long way from having any concept of women's liberation, and much of Bankers Life's advertising would be harshly judged today as being highly male chauvinistic in tone. For example, the following direct-mail advertisement had wide circulation in the late 1920s.

Below a picture of an attractive young woman who was quite obviously being used as a sex object was the following text:

> *Women are girls grown up!*
> *They'll always like the things they liked as girls—*
> *Good Times*
> *Good Clothes*
> *Pretty Things (Why not?)*
> *Flowers & Candy*
> *Etc., Etc., Etc.*
>
> *Today, no doubt, you're earning enough to buy yourself the Happiness of having these things.*
>
> *Tomorrow you may not be so fortunate.*
>
> *So you're interested in Life Insurance for yourself—*
>
> *Not, to be sure of leaving a lot of money for someone else, but rather, To be sure of having the money to buy Future Happiness when your earnings may lessen or cease. May we tell you more about Our Plan?*
>
>
>
> *Very truly yours,*
> *Bert N. Mills, Secretary*
> *The Bankers Life Company*
> *Des Moines, Iowa.*
>

The blotters and direct-mail advertising seemed to work. And so did the field agents, as hard for Jaeger and Nollen as they had worked for Kuhns. And their labors were reflected in the sales figures. After a slump in 1927 due to the Good Will Conversion Campaign, 1928 and 1929 were banner years: $886 million of insurance in force in 1928, $925 million in 1929.

The company had not attained its billion-dollar goal, as Kuhns had anticipated, when it reached its golden, fiftieth anniversary in June 1929, but it seemed to be, at most, only months away.

For some reason, perhaps in the hopes that the goal might be reached after the big push in June (President's Month) and in October (Policyholders' Month), the company decided to postpone its grand celebration until the following January. Unfortunately, October 1929

turned out to be something more than just Policyholders' Month for
Bankers Life. It is better known for being the Black Thursday month
for the New York stock market. On October 24, 1929, the blue sky of
the 1920s suddenly turned black and came crashing down.

When the agents and their wives came to Des Moines from all
over the nation on a cold January day in 1930 to celebrate the
company's golden anniversary, the nation's economy had already
gone into a deep freeze. But the company was determined that
nothing would chill this great celebration. At a banquet held for 1,600
people in the old Des Moines Coliseum, the largest formal banquet
ever held in Des Moines, on the evening of January 6, 1930, each diner
found beside his or her plate a ten-dollar gold piece—a gift from
President Nollen. No one then could fully appreciate how soon this
coin would become a collector's item, with the federal government
being the major collector.

Throughout the dinner and during the following two days of
school for the agents, a positive, booster spirit was maintained.
Bankers Life on its golden anniversary was about to enter its Golden
Age. The assembled agents solemnly promised to pass the $1 billion
mark in insurance in force before the end of that year, and Jaeger,
Jackman, and Nollen were there to tell them they could do it.

Actually the impact of the Depression did not hit the company
for another twelve months. The year 1930 did mark the highest point
in insurance in force in the company's history up to that time—$941
million. So close to the billion-dollar mark but not quite there. No
one in January 1930 could imagine that the goal still lay fifteen years
in the future.

By 1931 the slide downward had begun—only $913 million in
force. Then the descent became more rapid: $844 million in 1932,
$770 million in 1933, $734 million in 1934, and finally the bottom
reached, $723 million in 1935. In the year 1934 there was actually
more money going out in policy loans—$26 million—than was
coming in in premiums paid, $25 million. Thousands had to borrow
on their policies to feed their families; more thousands simply had to
let their policies lapse because they were unable to meet the premiums. Yet fortunately for the company, an even greater number
managed to hold on to their policies somehow, meeting their premium payments even if they had to forgo all simple luxuries and even
some of the basic necessities.

These were rough days for the home office. Certainly no
president in the history of the company ever had to cope with greater

difficulties than did Gerard Nollen. These were even rougher days for the field agents as commissions on new sales dwindled, and commissions on renewals began to vanish with the lapsed policies. The company had to finance many agents' office expenses in order to keep them in business at all.

Of perhaps even greater concern to the home office than the dwindling sales and lapsed policies was the state of its investments. When the old Association had been organized in 1879, it was restricted by its own Articles of Incorporation to invest its funds only in government bonds. But very early that restriction had been modified. As early as 1885, Bankers Life made its first farm loan of $2,800 at 6 percent interest on a farm in Guthrie County, Iowa. Very quickly, farm loans became the major area of investment for the company. In 1920, with assets at $44,450,000, Bankers Life had loans outstanding on farm mortgages amounting to $33,200,000 or about 75 percent of its total assets. By 1930 farm loans had increased to $67 million. It was then that serious trouble began. With corn selling at ten cents a bushel in 1932, farmers could no longer meet the interest payments, let alone try to pay anything on the principal. The inevitable consequence was foreclosure, with Bankers Life having to assume the ownership and management of the farms. In 1933, in Minnesota and Iowa alone, Bankers Life owned 711 farms. This necessitated an entire new operation, that of farm management, and the hiring of farm fieldmen to carry out the operation. These new employees were generally young men, although some were older, former county agents, who had received college training in agriculture. Among those hired straight out of the Iowa State Agricultural College at Ames was Herbert Pike, whose family had been in farming around Whiting, Iowa, since 1873.

Young Pike's letters to his family at home written soon after he accepted a position with Bankers Life provide a fascinating insight into both the kind of on-the-job training these young farm fieldmen received in 1933, and also into the state of agriculture in the dark days of the Depression. Pike was sent first into Texas, where the company had made a good many loans on ranches that were now in default, then to Minnesota, and finally to southern Iowa. Writing from Knoxville, Iowa, to his family in Whiting in 1935, Pike commented:

> *I like the rural people in southern Iowa—they have less income but more philosophy to fit the predicament. You wonder that Garret Versteegh is apparently satisfied with his*

lot. On one of our poor quarter sections in the rough southwest part of Mahaska County he raises sheep on shares and not much else. His headgear, whether it be the July straws, the November felt, or the January plaid, always has part of it flapping in his face, serving to cover up his grinning Pullman teeth—only one upper and two lowers left, but they mesh perfectly.

And again, writing from Ottumwa:

During the last week I have visited with the present fieldman (two territories are being divided into three), the farms in the southern four counties, and this week it is to be the farms in the remaining three counties. Southern Iowa is beset with problems which makes one dare to wonder why he could not have been left in a more familiar stomping ground like NW Iowa. For instance, there are very few grain elevators and crops must be peddled to neighbors and tenants, not always with the best of credit. The soil is a sickly yellow and subject to wash, the roads are steep, narrow and muddy after a heavy dew. It is essentially a cattle section where the most profitable returns are gotten from pasture and hay, corn and hogs having very little place. The farmers are a bit more easygoing, though likable, and one wonders why they are content here with the northern Iowa plains relatively close.

These young fieldmen under the general supervision of Joe Auner, a former banker in Algona, Iowa, who knew Iowa land and how to appraise it, were given instruction in how to rate the quality of land, from Grade A, choice, to Grade E, submarginal, how to assess the farm tenants' farming and managerial abilities—a far more subjective and difficult task, and how to search out potential buyers for the land Bankers Life held. Under Iowa law, no Iowa-based corporation could hold land taken on foreclosure for longer than five years, so the pressure on the field agents to sell land was as intense as was the company's concern to see that the farms were properly managed as long as the company held them.

The fieldmen were given a great deal of scientific information on soils, water table levels, erosion, crop rotation, and proper book-keeping. The agents in turn had to bring to their jobs not only technical information, but also a great deal of tact in dealing with farmers who had lost everything, and as Pike so clearly indicates, a sense of humor to make the job endurable. In his notes taken at a farm managers' meeting held at the home office in January 1936 with Frank Charlton and Auner, as head of the farm management and sales departments, Pike records his reactions to his job:

Selling Farms Without Neglecting Farm Management

It is evident that Mr. Charlton assigned this topic. Mr. Auner would have stated it, "Managing Farms Without Neglecting Sales." Apparently farm management is the most likely to be short-changed and for the "why" we might analyze some of the differences in the two jobs:

1. Aside from the bonus, a farm sale is more exciting than is management—it even gets in the papers.

2. Farm management is continuous, selling is an event and an end to management troubles on that farm (like the doctor, we can bury our mistakes).

3. Selling requires attention when prospect is ready, management can be put off.

Because it is the man who knows the farm best who can best sell it, the farm manager is the logical salesman. Different though the jobs are, they go hand in hand except as sales encroach upon the farm manager's time.

Pike then gives in his notes a summary of field servicing costs to Bankers Life and how the fieldman spent his ten-hour day of labor.

Field Servicing Costs

1. Fieldman:$150 per month, $6 per work day, 60¢ per hour

2. Steno:1/2 cost of fieldman's time, 30¢ per hour

3. Car: 3¢ per mile, plus 2¢ per mile for drivers' time

4. Telephone:1¢ a mile person-person call, ½¢ mile station-station

5. Personal Letter:Including your time, steno's time, stationery and postage—25¢ each.

6. Postcard:Short impersonal message 5¢ each.

Fieldman's Typical Day: 8 A.M. to 6 P.M. (10 hours)

Driving	Visiting	Lunch	Waiting for others	Transacting business
3 hours	1 hour	½ hour	1½ hours	4 hours

1. *Spends ⅓ time as a chauffeur.*
2. *1 hour visiting is time well spent.*
3. *Driving and waiting for people are the time-eaters.*

...The intensity of management given a farm must vary in proportion with the number of units handled by the farm manager. An acquaintance of mine has a full-time job managing only six farms—he is deeply concerned with depth of plowing, variety of seed and time of planting. Mr. Charlton is a farm manager, too, with over a thousand farms—he is interested only in results. And so our job lies somewhere between these two extremes.

The bonus that Pike mentions is a reference to a policy instituted by Bankers Life in September 1934 in order to push the sale of the some two thousand farms it held by foreclosure. The farm fieldmen, between September 1934 and January 1, 1935, were paid a bonus of 15¢ per acre, with a maximum of $50 for selling a farm. Although John Vanderlinden, head of farm investments, had been somewhat skeptical of such a bonus plan, Joe Auner and Frank Charlton had pushed this incentive plan, with apparently good results. To further stimulate farm sales, Auner published a little field journal, called *Our Farm Sales*, in which hints were given as to how to sell farms, and contests were run for the farm fieldmen to compete for prizes for selling the most farms. The techniques instituted by Kuhns, Mills, and Jaeger to sell insurance were now utilized to sell farms in Iowa, Minnesota, South Dakota, and Texas. Prices obtained ranged from $10 to $150 an acre, with the average price around $81 an acre for good Iowa land that some forty years later would be selling at $1,500 an acre.

Until the farm could be sold at what the company considered a fair price, it had to be properly managed and kept up. Farmers who had been in a depressed state for many years had not done much in the way of painting, roofing, or otherwise repairing their farm buildings which Bankers Life now possessed. In order to prevent deterioration and to aid sales, the company had to do a great deal of plant maintenance. It bought several carloads of paint, wholesale, for the painting of farm buildings. One of the favorite stories that is still told frequently at the home office concerns Bankers Life's massive farm painting operation. The paint that the company had purchased in bargain, wholesale lots was of a peculiar shade of yellow, unlike that used on farms anywhere else. Very quickly the company realized its error, for Bankers Life farms could now be spotted a mile away by the color of their buildings. Farmers in Wayne County, Iowa, or Pipestone County, Minnesota, would drive the county roads of their area and count off the number of Bankers Life farms. One favorite, if highly exaggerated, story told by farmers was that you could walk clear across Wayne County without ever stepping off a Bankers Life farm. Stories like these were not exactly the stuff out of which good public relations are made if one is trying to sell insurance to farmers and rural townsmen. Needless to say, the order quickly went out for a repainting of Bankers Life farms, this time to be done in the more traditional red for barns, white for farmhouses.

With the intense pressure exerted by Auner and Charlton on the farm fieldmen, the farms Bankers Life owned did get sold at a time when it was even more difficult to sell real estate than it was to sell life insurance. The company, desperately trying to rid itself of the many farms it had taken on foreclosure, had no desire certainly to acquire more farms through the default of payments on loans. It therefore welcomed a new policy in the early 1930s called "Grant of Possession." Under the terms of this program, a farmer who could not meet the interest and principal payments on his loans, could grant his creditor, in this case Bankers Life, to enter his farm and operate it by leasing it and then use the returns from this operation to pay taxes and upkeep, and whatever balance remained would then be applied on the interest and principal owed on the loan. In this way, the farmer did not lose his farm; he simply leased it to his creditor, and frequently the farmer himself would stay on the farm as a kind of tenant, on either a salaried or a crop share basis. Bankers Life, in turn, could often introduce more effective scientific farming techniques and would receive as much in return to satisfy the loan as it would have received if it had taken full ownership. And the company no longer had the obligation to make a quick sale. It was a highly satisfactory arrangement for both parties concerned.

The full onslaught of the Great Depression in 1932 had affected every phase of the insurance business as it did all other economic activities in the country. On the day that Franklin Roosevelt was inaugurated, March 4, 1933, every bank in the nation was closed and the banks would remain closed under the terms of the Emergency Banking Act until they could be inspected and declared sound by the federal government. This meant no checks could be cashed, or no cash withdrawals could be made. On March 13 President Nollen sent out an emergency message to the entire Bankers Life field force:

> *No doubt you all appreciate that the suspension of banking facilities has had two results affecting all life insurance companies. In the first place, the inability of policyholders and others to make regular payments to life insurance companies resulted in curtailing the current income of all companies. In the second place, the inability to get money from the banks resulted in such abnormally heavy demands for policy loans and cash surrender values that the demands cannot be met out of normal income. Therefore, in order to conserve the assets of life insurance companies and to avoid forcing a large volume of securities on the market which would have to be sold at a sacrifice detrimental to all life insurance policyholders and also to business in general, it was necessary to take emergency action when the bank suspension became nationwide....*

Nollen then outlined in detail just what this emergency action included: an extended grace period for the policyholder in the payment of premiums due, providing the policyholder requested and received authorization from the company for that grace period; the cessation of all policy loans or cash surrender value payments, ordered by the Iowa commissioner of insurance, until further notice; expected delays in payment of death benefits to beneficiaries; and the suspension of dividend payments for the present. Nollen attempted to conclude this solemn pronouncement on a more positive note: "President Roosevelt, in his inaugural address, very properly said that the thing we have most to fear is fear itself.... We need a universal war-time spirit of loyalty and service, a willingness to accept personal inconvenience as an unavoidable and vitally necessary element in winning this war against economic disorder."

But it was difficult not to be fearful in March 1933. With 14 million workers unemployed, hunger rode the land along with the desperate men in railroad box cars, along with the Okies and the Arkies in their beat-up jalopies, headed west to California, and along with the hundreds of thousands of youths hitching rides along Routes 1 and 6 and 30. Restless, jobless, suddenly rootless people moving somewhere, anywhere, in the hopes that maybe there was greener grass on the other side of some fence. But they couldn't find that fence. The whole nation was seared brown by nature's drought and by man's despair.

The first year of Roosevelt's administration did bring an abrupt change in the nation's mood. The federal government was at last taking action, and although unemployment remained high, the people's hopes were raised. And with the emergency relief measures, there came a renewed belief that recovery might be possible. Of all of the various interest groups affected by the Depression, it was the farmers who received the most immediate and greatest assistance from the New Deal. And because Bankers Life had always been closely linked with the rural Midwest, the improved lot of the farmer could not help but have a beneficial effect upon Bankers Life.

The Great Depression, however, was an economic illness so acute that it could not be quickly cured by political remedies no matter how vigorously they were applied. Some of the sharpest pain had been alleviated by Frazier-Lemke Moratorium on foreclosures, by the Agricultural Adjustment Act, and by the Federal Emergency Relief Administration, but the economic malignancy still persisted.

For Bankers Life, the worst year of the Depression was dependent upon which yardstick one used to measure. In terms of new business, the bottom year was 1933, when the total sales figure for all agencies was only $42,322,488. Although the assets of the company never declined throughout the Depression, the year of the smallest increase in assets was 1934, when they increased only $7 million over the previous year. In terms of the amount of insurance in force, the bottom was reached in 1935, with only $723 million of insurance in force, a drop of $11 million from the previous year. That long-sought billion-dollar goal, so nearly achieved in 1930, was now a long way off. For premium income received, the worst year for Bankers Life was 1937, when only $24,651,068 was taken in.

This decade of depression greatly affected the policies, products, and procedures of the company. The amount of insurance a person could buy was once again severely limited by company policy, for no life insurance company wanted to sell a $300,000 policy on a person's life. They were the so-called jumbo risks, where the temptation for suicide or for murder by one's beneficiaries might prove to be too great to resist.

The company, along with most other life insurance companies, also drastically changed its disability riders during the years of the Depression. The disability rider feature had been adopted in the late

1920s by Bankers Life and it had immediately proved to be a major stimulant to sales. Bankers Life offered two types of disability riders. One was called "preferred disability" and was offered to the professional man. It provided for the payment of disability income—$10 per each $1,000 worth of insurance—in the event that the professional man could not continue in his vocation: the surgeon who could not use his right hand, for example, or the trial lawyer who lost his ability to speak. The other disability rider, providing for the same payment, was offered to the general public, but in this case, the disability had to be total, not simply an impairment that prevented the insured from pursuing his or her particular profession. These disability features had been so popular in the market and had been so vigorously pushed by the insurance salesmen that it was often said the sales agent was in reality selling disability coverage and simply threw the life insurance in for good measure.

In 1931, however, $10 loomed very large indeed. So many policyholders were claiming either professional or total disability that the company was forced, over the violent objections of their salesmen, to drastically change the disability feature on new business sold. For the "preferred disability" rider, there would be hereafter only a $5 payment per $1,000 of insurance, and for the general disability rider, there would be no payment at all, only a waiver of premium. In each case, on all new policies, there had to be a six-month waiting period to make sure the disability was permanent.

In 1930, just at the onset of the Depression, Bankers Life had introduced two new policy plans: a Life Retirement Plan and a Family Protection Policy. The first of these two new policies produced few sales. People were not much interested in retirement in 1932, just in survival. The Family Protection Plan, however, had great appeal. By providing for greater benefits during the earlier years when a man needed more protection for his dependent children, this policy became a big seller during the Depression years. Bankers Life also permitted for the first time ever monthly payment of premiums on all of its policies.

There were organizational changes in these years as well. More and more agency managers were agreeable to signing new contracts which made them branch officer managers, compensated mainly by salaries not by commissions. Even though by doing so they might lose some of their former independence which they had enjoyed as agency managers, many in these Depression years preferred a regular monthly income to the once glittering but now not so promising hope of big renewal commissions in the future.

In order to keep many of their branch offices open, the company increasingly had to make loans to their managers. Some of these large loans were carried on the books for years. One agency manager, for example, who had begun selling for Bankers Life in 1920, was during the Depression years nearly $50,000 in debt to the company. This debt, which after 1932 was interest-free, was slowly reduced over the next four decades, but at the time of his death in 1972, the former agent still owed the company over $800. Bill Jaeger, and later Marvin Lewis, as agency vice-president, and John Grimes, Mills's former assistant who became superintendent of agency administration, during this long interim had repeatedly come to the agent's assistance by extending his loans and helping him put his own financial house in order so that he could make monthly payments against his indebtedness. Bankers Life could hardly be accused of not taking care of its own force with an almost maternal solicitude.

Although it was the salesmen in the field who had to face the full brunt of the Depression's force, the home office staff did not remain unaffected financially. Office personnel was reduced, and everyone earning a salary over $1,500 per annum had his salary reduced by 10 percent, effective April 1, 1933. This reduction continued until January 1935.

In the hopes of boosting sales, Bankers Life for the first time in its history turned to an outside advertising agency in 1934 to start a program of advertising in magazines with a national circulation. Upon the advice of John Brine, president of the Rollins Hosiery Mills in Des Moines and later a member of the Bankers Life Board of Directors, the company signed a contract with the William D'Arcy advertising agency in St. Louis, and soon Bankers Life ads began to appear first in *The Saturday Evening Post*, later in *Business Week*, *Time*, and *Life*, bearing the slogan "Bankers Life of Des Moines—the Company with a Surplus of Safety." It was heartening to talk of a surplus of anything in 1934. Quite naturally, the field agents were delighted with the decision of the company to follow Metropolitan's and Prudential's lead and go into national advertising. Many of these salesmen expected a miracle in sales as soon as the first *Saturday Evening Post* advertisement appeared, but as John Grimes observed, "Miracles they didn't get." Nevertheless, this advertising campaign did a great deal to boost the sales force's morale, and it unquestionably helped to achieve a greater name recognition from a national public.

The sales force had other reasons to be grateful to the home office during these Depression years in addition to the national advertising campaign. Heretofore, the company, like most other insurance companies, had done little to train its salesmen in selling techniques. It did not even have a training manual until Merwyn Cramer, as a young subagent in Lincoln, Nebraska, developed one in 1927. In 1932, however, at the prompting of Bill Jaeger, Nollen agreed to hire a young graduate from the Wharton School of Finance, Ben H. Williams, as the company's first educational training director. By the summer of 1934, Williams was ready to open his first school for newly recruited salesmen. These "first schools," beginning with Minneapolis, were held in agency center cities throughout the country, with very mixed results, depending in part upon the cooperation and enthusiasm of the agency manager in each area. It was not until George Harper joined the educational department as an assistant to Williams that the format and content of these instructional sessions were standardized and the quality of instruction was improved. Roy Frowick, who succeeded Harper, proved to be an even more effective teacher who quickly won the support of agency managers and new recruits throughout the company.

Nollen's record of innovations supportive of the field agents is in many ways as impressive as that of Kuhns, but in addition, Nollen was greatly concerned, as Kuhns had not been, in improving the general welfare and morale of the home office personnel. In 1923 he had obtained Board approval for a very modest pension plan for home office staff over Nourse's vigorous objection. Although this plan had to be suspended in 1935, it was reinstituted in 1940 with a formal pension, death benefit, and disability plan followed by a hospital and surgical plan in 1942.

The depression decade of the 1930s was the most difficult period in the company's history since the first year or two after conversion from an association to a mutual legal reserve company. Yet from Nollen on down to the newest stenographer, no one in the home office ever seemed to doubt that the company would survive. Nor did a sense of panic pervade the top floors of the Liberty Building. In many respects, life went on in much the same routine as that which had prevailed in the 1920s. The top officers of the company continued to meet every noon at their customary rendezvous, one particular round table in the old Des Moines Club, for lunch after a hard morning of work that for many had begun before eight o'clock. After lunch, some retired to the game room for a game of pitch or bridge, or, weather permitting, followed Jaeger's lead to the Wakonda Club golf links. Even with all of the problems that the Depression had presented, McConney and Grimes would not later remember these years as having been filled with unbearable pressures or ulcer-producing anxieties.

These dark years of depression should be remembered as years of successful innovations: new products, better training in sales techniques for the field force, a revised rate book schedule based upon a 3 percent interest rate instead of the 3½ percent that had prevailed since 1911. Both the quality and the quantity of advertising and intracompany publications improved. It was in these years that Mills came up with "Double Duty Dollars" which quickly replaced D'Arcy's "Surplus of Safety" slogan. "Double Duty," as the accompanying literature made clear, was a reference to the fact that when one bought a life insurance policy from Bankers Life, his dollars did double duty—they bought protection and they bought dividends through wise investments. "Double Duty Dollars" proved to be one of the most effective advertising lines and identification slogans in the company's history.

By 1938 the worst of the Depression was past. The amount of insurance in force was back up to $752 million, and premium income showed its first increase since 1930. The company no longer had to be preoccupied with merely holding its defense line. It could once again begin to think in terms of an aggressive advance: of the possibility of entering new fields of insurance, and more immediately of building its own home office building after sixty years of renting space.

At the annual meeting held in Des Moines in April 1938, one of the policyholders, Judge Charles Hutchinson, arose and asked permission to speak. This was unprecedented, and none of the officers knew what to expect. Hutchinson quickly reassured them by stating that he was taking the liberty on behalf of all the policyholders to thank President Nollen for "the quite satisfactory manner in which the affairs of the company have been conducted" during these recent unpleasant times. To that sentiment, agents, officers, and directors might all have added a hearty amen.

5/Bankers Life
Builds New Structures

1939-1954

By the summer of 1938 the Depression for the first time in seven years was no longer the all-absorbing topic of conversation in America. We had passed through the Biblical seven years of Famine. We were now ready psychologically for the seven years of feast. We had not, to be sure, turned Mr. Hoover's metaphorical corner around which, he had promised us as far back as 1931, prosperity lay, but at least we could now see that corner. Unemployment was still too high, and the consumer price index remained considerably below that of 1929, but for those companies that had survived the Depression with some reserve capital, these lingering vestiges of the Depression were now a stimulant to expansion, not a deterrent. Unemployment meant cheap labor; deflated prices meant inexpensive construction material. The year 1938 was a good year to consider building before everyone else got the same idea and we found ourselves pushed around that corner into prosperity and high prices.

Bankers Life was one of those companies that, all things considered, had survived the seven lean years without becoming totally emaciated. Although the company had suffered serious declines both in the total amount of insurance in force and in premium income, its assets even in the worst years had never dropped but instead had risen each year, if only slightly. By the end of 1937 these assets stood at $216,265,043. The insurance in force had shown an encouraging increase of nearly $16 million over the previous year, and although premium income was at the lowest point it had been since 1925, there was every indication that this decline would be reversed in

91

the coming year. It was President Nollen's considered judgment that 1938 should be the year to begin construction of a home for Bankers Life.

For nearly sixty years, Bankers Life had been a tenant in Des Moines. Beginning with a back room in the old Des Moines Bank at Third and Walnut streets, over the next six decades, the company had had seven different rented homes, but for at least twenty years, ever since Kuhns had assumed the presidency, the chief officers of the company had dreamed of having a home they could call their own. As soon as World War I was over, and private construction was again possible, Kuhns had begun planning for the construction of a home office building. Then, as detailed earlier, he had become involved with Nothstine in the construction of the Liberty Building. Under the terms of that final arrangement with Nothstine, Kuhns had committed the company to a fifteen-year lease with the managers of the Liberty Building, and from 1924 until 1939, Bankers Life would be under contractual obligation to rent the top five (ultimately seven) floors of that building.

But Kuhns not only thought big, he thought long—far into the future. The fifteen-year lease in no way precluded his planning for a home office building and preferably one that would be located outside of the coal-smoke grime and increasingly car-clogged streets of downtown Des Moines. In 1925 Bankers Life bought a large tract of land, consisting of nearly a full city block at Thirty-first and Grand Avenue. This was in the very center of the city's fine old residential district. Grand Avenue was appropriately named—it was the grand thoroughfare of western Des Moines. From the Hubbell Mansion, Terrace Hill, at Twenty-third and Grand, on westward for the next twenty blocks were the great homes of Des Moines, terminating at Forty-second Street with the impressive stone, baronial mansion of Senator Francis. Bankers Life clearly would be moving into a very exclusive neighborhood.

Even if the company had not been tied to the Liberty Building for the next fifteen years, the high cost of construction in the late 1920s, immediately followed by the disastrous Depression of the 1930s, would probably have delayed construction for a decade and a half anyway. Now, however, the Liberty Building lease would soon be terminated, and Nollen was ready to pick up the Kuhns dream and make it a reality.

Nollen, in addition, had his own reasons for wanting to complete the home office building during his presidency. His company and he personally had long been in friendly rivalry with Des Moines' other major insurance company, Equitable Life of Iowa, over which his brother Henry presided. As soon as Henry Nollen was elected president of Equitable in 1921, plans were begun for the construction of a new Equitable building at the southwest corner of Locust and Sixth. Designed by the local architectural firm of Proud-foot, Bird and Rawson, this eighteen-story brick structure, topped by a seven-story white terra-cotta Gothic finial, which housed the elevator motors and a water reservoir, was completed in 1924. It was the only building in Des Moines that might be called a skyscraper. The architects had clearly borrowed heavily in both concept and detail from the Woolworth Building in lower Manhattan, which at that time was the world's tallest building. Although less than half the height of its New York counterpart, the Equitable Building, particularly at night when its tower was illuminated by spotlights, dominated the Des Moines skyline.

Built at a cost of $3 million, it was also the city's most expensive building. But the company got full value for its money, not only in the office space it provided Equitable on the top five floors and in the rent received from doctors, lawyers, and shopkeepers in the remaining thirteen floors, but also in terms of public relations. No other company in the state had such a magnificently impressive advertising billboard. Although the company occupied less than one third of the building, it was still in the public's mind the "Equitable Building." Any insurance company that could spend that much on a building and occupy that much space must be as solid as Prudential's Rock of Gibraltar. Bankers Life had nearly twice as much insurance in force in 1925 as did Equitable of Iowa, but nine out of ten people in Des Moines if asked what was the city's largest insurance company, would have answered without hesitation, "Why, Equitable, of course." Gerard Nollen was eager to present as imposing a facade to his brother Henry and to the people of Des Moines as did Equitable.

Nollen had been quite content originally simply to follow up on Kuhns's plans and to build at the Grand Avenue site. The location greatly appealed to him. Two miles away from the downtown's polluted air, only two blocks away from his own home at Twenty-ninth and Grand Avenue, it was an ideal setting. But those members of the Board who were local businessmen, Ross Clemens, Vernon Clark, and John Brine, applied pressure on Nollen for the company to stay downtown. In so doing, they were obviously influenced by downtown merchants—Younker Brothers, the city's largest department store, in particular—and by the many restaurant and garage owners who were not happy over the prospect of losing the patronage of some five hundred Bankers Life employees. It was pointed out to Nollen that if the home office were located far out on Thirty-first Street and Grand, the company would have to build its own cafeteria and run its own parking lot. To this barrage of arguments, Nollen finally succumbed. He agreed to construct the new building in the center city, although as McConney, who quite obviously wanted the Grand Avenue location, points out in his *Reminiscences*, ultimately the company had to do downtown just what it thought it was avoiding by not moving out to Grand — it had to build its own cafeteria and manage its own very large parking lot.

Having decided to remain within the downtown loop area, Nollen then had to find an available site. The company, during the Depression, had taken possession of a few lots on High Street, between Seventh and Eighth streets. High Street, as the name implies, runs along the crest of a small hill in downtown Des Moines, parallel to but somewhat higher in elevation than Grand Avenue, one block to the south. Because of the large number of churches located in the immediate vicinity, this elevated area had long been known as Piety Hill—a not inappropriate name for the location of a company that had long prided itself on its moral integrity. To obtain enough land in the block in addition to the lots the company already owned, Bankers Life would have to buy out several other occupants, including a small suboffice of the Northwestern Bell Telephone Company, the Central Presbyterian Church, and a lovely old home which had been the Weitz family homestead. These properties were quickly acquired at a cost of $157,850. The Central Presbyterian congregation in particular was pleased to receive $78,750 for its old and inadequate building. It could now build the new church it had long wanted out on Thirty-eighth and Grand, not far from the site where Bankers Life had once planned to build.

On November 3, 1937, the Board of Directors authorized payment for these properties and two weeks later it appointed Nollen "with such other officers in the Company as he may select" to serve as an architectural selection committee and to appoint a building committee "and such other committees as he deems advisable." On December 6 Nollen appointed an Executive Committee, consisting of himself as chairman, Jaeger, Fowler, and McConney, "to act as the central authority in delegating responsibility and making decisions in the matter of contract approvals and general procedure." In addition, he appointed McConney, chairman, J. S. Corley and R. W. Hatton to serve on a Building Construction Committee, and also Jaeger, chairman, along with D. N. Warters, G. A. Parks, and E. A. Beck for the Furnishing and Equipment Committee.

The first basic issue the Executive Committee had to resolve was the size and use of the building. Should the company build a structure far in excess of its present needs and rent out a large portion of that building until such time as it would need an increasingly larger portion of the building? This is what Equitable had done. Or should Bankers Life build only for its present needs but with a design that would allow expansion as future space requirements warranted. The committee quickly decided that it would not follow Equitable's example but would build only for Bankers Life, which would be the sole occupant. Quite wisely, Nollen opposed getting into the office leasing business. He had seen the difficulties his brother Henry had had getting tenants out as Equitable needed room for expansion and also of getting tenants in during the years of depression when some of the building's office space had gone begging. The Bankers Life Building, unlike the Equitable Building, would be wholly committed to one enterprise.

The second issue that had to be quickly resolved, of course, was the choice of an architectural firm. The Executive Committee made an excellent choice in the local Des Moines firm of Tinsley, McBroom and Higgins, with Leland McBroom serving as the chief architect for the project. Arthur H. Neumann and Brothers, also of Des Moines, was awarded the general contractor contract.

Elaborate tests were conducted to determine the weight-bearing potential of the soil. Some of these test holes went down as deep as eighty feet. It was discovered that under the ground surface there was a fifteen-foot layer of clay and then an equally deep layer of sand and gravel. Below these two strata was another narrow layer of clay followed by more sand and gravel and finally fifty feet down a bedrock of blue shale. Load-bearing tests showed the soil would support a downward thrust of ten thousand pounds per square foot with little or no settlement. On the basis of these tests, the architects decided that they could dispense with expensive pilings and instead, by borrowing an idea used by Frank Lloyd Wright for his massive Imperial Hotel in earthquake-prone Tokyo, use relatively inexpensive concrete footings. This resulted in a considerable saving in the total cost of construction.

In June and July 1938 the existing structures in the block were razed. On Monday, August 29, Gerard Nollen turned the first spadeful of dirt, and excavation began. In all 44,200 cubic yards of dirt were removed, creating "the biggest hole ever dug in the state of Iowa," as one Bankers Life promotional pamphlet proudly announced. The excavation crew worked by day and also by night under brilliant floodlights to the fascination of hundreds of interested spectators for whom the company had obligingly built a "Kibitzer's Gallery." Newly perfected metal forms, instead of the more orthodox and more expensive wooden forms, were used for the foundation walls, which added to the strength and waterproofness of the foundation.

The Executive Committee quite properly had given the architects great freedom in the basic design of the structure. The only feature it insisted that the architects take into consideration was in the design of the general work space on each floor. As McConney told the Des Moines Real Estate Operators meeting in September 1938:

> *An additional reason for ... [Bankers Life] building its own home office is the fact that the usual office building is built for small units and it has been traditional to build with a lot of columns in the building, seventeen feet to eighteen feet apart. Insurance work is handled by large groups so we need large open rooms with very few dividing walls, and in the Liberty Building (for example, the sixth and seventh floors) you can see how uneconomical and inefficient it is to have columns standing all over the room and getting in the way especially when a department becomes crowded.*

This demand for great open work spaces with no columns determined the skeletal structure of the building. From the first through the fifth floors, steel beams spanned the 55½-foot width of the rooms without any intermediate column supports for the entire 235-foot length of the rooms. This not only provided complete flexibility in the use of the work areas but it also created a feeling of space and openness that was psychologically appealing to both the workers in the offices and visitors.

The executive offices, more traditionally divided by partitioning walls, were on the sixth floor. Above that was a penthouse, containing a handsome Board of Directors room, a foyer, and a small consulting office. For the outer skin of the building—and it was just that, a containing skin or facade that had no structure support function—the architects chose Minnesota rainbow granite, so called for its beautiful variegated coloring ranging from light pink to jet black, for the first 23 feet above grade, and for the remaining 122 feet,

Bedford limestone from Indiana. At the center rear of the building, taking up about one-half the length of the entire building and rising two stories in height, was the auditorium, and beneath it, the gymnasium for home office employees to use for physical fitness workouts during the lunch hour and after work.

Construction went on all through the winter of 1938–39. On May 29, 1939, the granite cornerstone was laid, containing a sealed copper box which held copies of the *Des Moines Register and Tribune* for that date, photographs of the officers of the company, various Bankers Life publications and sales literature, and copies of the Board of Directors resolutions authorizing the construction of the building and the employment of the architects. Ten months later, in March 1940, Bankers Life moved out of the Liberty Building, which had been its home for fifteen years, into its impressive new mansion. A future president of Bankers Life, Robert Houser, at that time had a temporary part-time job with the company to earn money for his college tuition, and it was his task to carry the officers' inkwells over to the new building.

On April 13, 1940, the building was formally dedicated, and with great pride the home office was open to the public for open-house tours. The architects and Bankers Life had good reason to be proud. Rising 145 feet above ground level, the building, including the auditorium, covered 33,875 square feet. It would never dominate the skyline as Equitable did. Indeed it would eventually be completely overshadowed by the thirty-four-story Ruan building a block away. But it contained 100,000 square feet of the most functional office space in the city. Outwardly, it presented an appearance of modernity and strength, exactly the image that the company would want to present to the public. It had none of the elaborate ornamentation of Equitable's medievel Gothic tower, anachronistically placed in twentieth-century Iowa, but neither did it present the unrelieved starkness of the later glass, concrete, and metal box architecture of the 1960s and 1970s. It was as the architects said, "modified modernism," and it has stood the test of time well.

The architects had wanted not just functionalism. They also wanted and they got just enough abstract and stylized ornamentation to add beauty to functional form. From the moment the visitor approaches the main entrance on High Street, his eye is attracted to the marble retaining wall, which is repeated in the first story of the building. Above the three entrance doors are the stunning, molded glass panels, executed by two midwestern artists, Lowell Houser and

Glenn Chamberlain. The artists' drawings for these panels had already been submitted to the architects and the Executive Committee when McConney spoke to the Des Moines Real Estate Operators in September 1938, and clearly he was forewarning the general public for their appearance when he said:

> *Modern architecture depends on design and line so that the exterior only has a little decoration, as for example over the main entrance. Therefore, we have to do something for the main entrance—we don't know yet what it will be. Bronze plaques of the early pioneers in a penny-pinching attitude are not very attractive—symbols of tall corn and agriculture have been tried over and over again in every government building— the mother protecting orphan children has been used for everything from insurance to mouth wash.*
>
> *The other day an idea came along and I would like to know what you practical businessmen would think of some decoration conveying this thought.*
>
> *Out here in the Great Plains for thousands of years the Indians were content to worship, shall we say, the elements— Earth, Fire, and Water. Earth from which they got their food, on which they lived and walked. Fire, a warm shield against the cold, a light in darkness to show him to friends and warn him of his foes and around it was his social life. Water, which by quenching thirst quickened life; it fed the rivers and lakes on which he traveled and provided stores of fishes.*
>
> *A hundred fifty years ago came the white men over the Alleghenies and in that short span of time he has harnessed those elements of Earth, Fire, and Water. By his tenacity, his urge to go forward, and his love of power over nature, he has given us our agriculture, our forges and factories, our water power, and enabled us to sail on the water. What would you think of something to symbolize that idea?*

What the realty men may have thought is not a matter of record, but fortunately the architects and the Executive Committee thought well of it. And so the great panels were executed, each with a giant Indian figure bearing the symbols of the elements and below each Indian, nude white male figures deriving benefits of civilization from the natural elements which the Indians had once possessed. These panels are masterpieces of late 1930 modern art deco. A minor contretemps arose over the question as to whether the totally nude figures might offend public sensibilities, but happily, the artists won out over the committee's fear of Mrs. Grundy, and the figures appear as designed, sans fig leaves.

Even the small details of design were carefully considered and successfully resolved by the architects: the handsome brass ornamentation on the elevator doors, the sloping of window ledges so that they would not be cluttered with junk, the recessing of the windows so as to shade them from a hot summer sun and by so doing also giving the horizontal form of the building interesting vertical lines that lessened its blocklike appearance. The stairs were all built of Virginia greenstone, which is skidproof, thus making matting unnecessary. Attention was given even to the toilet stalls which were suspended from the ceiling to make it easy to clean the lavoratory floors.

Less apparent to the casual visitor are the many innovations for the mechanical operations of the building. The walls were all insulated with two inches of cork. The architects were a generation ahead of their time in the conservation of energy; and also in their concern for pollution. The air is filtered through an electrostatic precipitator which removes 90 percent of all impurities. The atmospheric control system of central heating and air conditioning that was installed was far in advance of its time. This system consisted of two major elements—a perimeter warming and cooling system of continuous one-inch copper pipes in all exterior walls within whose envelope the centralized air-conditioning system of Freon compressors (for cooling) and hot water (for heating) operated.

The leading journal for the profession, *Architectural Record*, devoted nearly its entire June 1940 issue to the Bankers Life Building. In a lead editorial, entitled "Once in a Great While," the journal paid it homage:

> *Perhaps every decade or so—a farsighted and fortunate architect finds an equally farsighted client with whom he is able to work in so unhampered and constructive a way that the resultant building actually sets a new standard and serves as a challenge to all concerned with architectural progress. In the judgment of* Record *editors, such architects were Tinsley, McBroom and Higgins; such a client was the Bankers Life Company; and such a building is the new home office of this insurance company in Des Moines, Iowa.*
>
> *The basic problem involved was to design a building "for economical and efficient line production of insurance policies under the most favorable conditions possible for the*

workers within the building." Analyzed as whole or in part,
the building shows how successfully the architects met this
challenge....

We devote unusual space to this project, not because we
feel that a large number of our readers will have the oppor-
tunity of designing an insurance company's home office build-
ing, but because the architects have successfully solved so
many specialized problems which cut across all commercial
buildings.

The *Architectural Record* completed its tribute to the home office
building by naming it the best building of the decade. Bankers Life
had waited for sixty years for a home of its own. It had been worth the
wait.

Just as Bankers Life had quickly filled up its unused office space in its
new quarters in the Liberty Building in 1924 by jumping into the
operation of a radio station, so now sixteen years later it was to do the
same in its new home office building by making the big decision to go
into group insurance. In many respects, this decision was so momentous as to rank second in importance in the company's history only to
the decision in 1911 to change from an assessment association to a
legal mutual reserve company.

The decision to enter group insurance was a long time in
gestation. As early as 1926, the Board of Directors had approved of a
resolution offered by W. O. Finkbine "to authorize the officers of the
Company to establish rules for the acceptance of new insurance on
the group basis recently announced by the Company and called the
'Easy Payment Plan.'" Applications would be considered without
examination on groups of ten or more, not to exceed $2,500 on any
one life for persons between the ages of eighteen and forty-five
inclusive. Apparently this plan envisaged the formation of voluntary
groups, not necessarily the employees of a single company or enterprise. The Easy Payment Plan had a moderate degree of success up
until the time of depression, but it remained an individual policy
program on a group basis rather than a true group insurance program.

By the time Bankers Life began to consider seriously the
question of entering group insurance in the late 1930s, there were
twenty-one companies that dominated the field, each having at least
$25 million worth of group insurance in force. Of these, Metropolitan
was the giant, with nearly $4 billion worth of group insurance in

force, followed by Equitable of New York, Travelers, Aetna, and Prudential, each with around $1.5 billion in force. The remaining sixteen companies had amounts ranging from $400 million down to $25 million.

All of the larger companies belonged to the Group Association, an organization not unlike the old pooling associations among railroads and within the iron and steel industry in the 1870s and 1880s. This Association essentially policed the group insurance business and determined policy and procedure by setting premium rates, group policy provisions, and sales tactics. Any company in the group insurance business that violated the Association's regulations was forced out of the Association and its future prospects would not be very bright. As Dennis Warters, who made an exhaustive study of group insurance for Bankers Life, pointed out in his memorandum:

> *Competition among the companies [in the Association] centered on minor details in the contracts and the probable amount of the premium refund or dividend to be paid to the policyholder. Even when so limited, competition was intense as the buyer was served by a highly competent staff of accountants, lawyers, etc., rather expert in comparing proposals.*

In preparation for his report to the Board, Warters made the wise decision to consult with his fellow actuaries concerned with group insurance in some of the largest companies: Metropolitan, Aetna, Connecticut General, Lincoln National, and Blue Cross. To each he asked the basic question, Should Bankers Life enter the group insurance field at this time? The response he received was very mixed. Four of those consulted said yes, four said no, and one, Eddy of Connecticut General, said that he was unable to give a definite answer—the pros and cons were too nearly balanced. The arguments Warters received for entering the field included: (1) a social responsibility that large insurance companies had to the public by providing insurance at a lower distribution cost and also to their own agents in providing additional business and a higher income; (2) the broadening of company and agency contacts and providing excellent name advertising; (3) providing a psychological stimulant for the agents by giving them additional products to offer their customers; and (4) providing the agents with excellent leads for individual life insurance. The arguments against entering the field were also persuasive:

(1) Social Security does now and will increasingly limit the future prospects for group insurance; (2) the federal government is considering and may soon adopt a national accident and health insurance plan which will destroy that area of group insurance; (3) the field is adequately covered now by the present companies and the competition is already intense; (4) the present rates on some forms of group insurance are too low to meet expenses and claims.

As to the returns received from the various divisions of the group insurance field, Warters discovered after a great deal of diligent poking around and asking the right questions that group life was profitable, as was group accident and health. Group hospitalization was questionable while group annuities were actually sold at a loss by most companies simply to satisfy customer demand.

After considering all of these responses and data, Warters presented his report to the Board on December 30, 1940. His own recommendation was quite unequivocal. Bankers Life should enter all areas of the group insurance field. The Board received the report with great interest, but at Nollen's suggestion took no formal action at that moment. Although Nollen was quite obviously sympathetic to Warters' recommendation, he realized that the question of entering the group field had badly divided his staff. McConney and Warters were enthusiastic proponents, but Jaeger was violently opposed. Warters, in his listing of arguments in support of group insurance, had attempted to stress the advantages of group insurance for the agents in the field, but Jaeger was unconvinced. He saw group insurance as a direct threat to individual life and annuity programs, and he was sure that nine out of ten of his agents would feel the same way. Jaeger, as usual, was bluntly direct. Bankers Life, he told Nollen and the Board, would enter the group field only over his dead body.

Nollen must not have found it easy to move in direct opposition to the adamant position taken by his loyal lieutenant, but Nollen, after all, was the commander and Jaeger only the lieutenant. The decision had to be Nollen's, and it seemed to him that the arguments for entering the group field were too compelling to ignore. Just as his brother Henry Nollen had seen in 1910 that conversion from an assessment association to a mutual legal reserve company could not be delayed even if individual egos might be bruised by such action, so now three decades later, Gerard Nollen saw that the future success of the company lay with group insurance no matter how vigorously Jaeger and his agents might oppose it.

At a meeting on January 13, 1941, two weeks after Warters had presented his report, the Board authorized Bankers Life to issue contracts for life, accident, health, annuity, and hospital insurance on a group basis. Jaeger, as expected, voted no. When the vote went overwhelmingly against him, Jaeger announced that although he couldn't stop the company from making a bad decision, he would be goddamned if any of his agents had anything to do with group insurance.

Jaeger's opposition to group insurance was not due to a basic intransigent opposition toward change per se. He ordinarily welcomed new ideas and new products from the actuarial department. But he had investigated the whole group insurance field and had come to a quite different conclusion as to its effect upon the field agents from that of Warters. In the first place, group insurance was a very special field, requiring its own kind of training, sales promotion, and field contacts. The individual life agent would find it difficult to retool himself for group insurance. More important, the field agent, even if he were successful in finding and selling a group contract to a company, had no assurance that he would get the commission, for the employer/client who was providing group insurance benefits for his employees usually demanded and got the right to name the agency who would get the commission for the sale, and frequently the agency or broker named would be someone who had not done any of the initial work in the sale at all. Moreover, most companies involved in group insurance had found it advantageous to depend heavily on insurance brokers. Bankers Life had traditionally avoided the broker, preferring instead its own field force which dealt exclusively in Bankers Life insurance. For all of these reasons, Jaeger knew that the resentment among his agents would be intense, and he was not mistaken in his judgment.

One of the few field agents who supported the group insurance program from its inception was Merwyn Cramer. Cramer in the past ten years had moved up the sales force ladder from being a subagent for the W. I. Fraser agency in Lincoln, Nebraska, to becoming agency manager in Los Angeles. At a meeting held in California in late January soon after the Board had made its decision, Nollen, who was in attendance, asked Cramer, with only twelve hours' notice, to present a paper to the agents assembled on "Why Bankers Life Should Enter the Group Insurance Business." Cramer was a dynamic personality and an effective speaker, but it is doubtful that even he was able to win many converts among these old-line individual life agents. Clearly Bankers Life would have to assemble an entirely new field force if it was to compete effectively in the group insurance field.

The recruiting of a group insurance force proved to be no easy task, for by 1941, with much of the world at war and with America's adoption of its first peacetime military draft and its feverish preparations for a war that now seemed inevitable, the Depression of the 1930s was truly over and labor was scarce. As a first step in building a group insurance force, the company appointed Walter Bjorn, who proved to be a fortunate choice. No one was more knowledgeable of the group field than was Bjorn. He came to Bankers Life from his most recent position as actuary for Blue Cross in New York City, but prior to that he had served for ten years as group actuary and sales assistant in the group term and casualty department of Connecticut General. By training he was an actuary, but by temperament and preference he was a salesman, and while at Connecticut General he had earned the nickname of the "Viking," for his proclivity to roam the country seeking new sales for large group cases.

Bjorn was made head of the group department, reporting directly to Warters. It was his task to assemble a sales force and to make the initial contacts for potential customers, a task that Bjorn thoroughly enjoyed. From inside the company, Jack Archibald was assigned the responsibility for group products and with it, the responsibility of developing and filing group insurance forms with state insurance departments. Bill Rae and Art Roberts were transferred from the program development department into the group division. These officers and their secretaries made up the entire home office staff in the beginning. To recruit an experienced field force demanded all of Bjorn's knowledge of the field and all of his dynamic persuasiveness. He was handicapped by the strict ethics then (but no longer) observed within the life insurance industry which forbade one company from attempting to lure away an employee or agent of another company without that company's permission. Jaeger, who had vowed that none of his agents would go into group sales, insisted that this ethical standard be observed in respect to the agents of other companies. As a result, Bjorn had to build his initial sales force, as Warters would later recall in his *Early History of Bankers Life Group Department*, from men who

> a. in their own opinion were not receiving proper recognition or were stymied behind others of approximately the same age;

b. *individualists who had been discharged for failure to obey personnel rules...;*

c. *extreme egoists who were rarely discouraged and believed in their own ability to overcome any and every obstacle.*

It was a motley, freebooting crew that the Viking assembled for this first expedition into the dangerous group insurance waters, but it proved to be an amazingly effective one.

One reason for the crew's initial success was that it was sailing under a carefully designed operational plan, one that Warters and Bjorn had designed in order to avoid the reefs and shoals and the hostile shore artillery of the old established companies. Again, Warters, in his history, gives a sparse but revealing outline of that plan:

> *With the assistance of Walt, we carefully studied various ways in which we might build a successful group operation and adopted the following plan.*
>
> a. *Employ at least four experienced group representatives, locating one in the head office in Des Moines and the others in New York, Chicago and Los Angeles as regional group managers. We decided to offer them a salary plus an attractive incentive bonus based on production.*
>
> b. *Stay out of the Group Association and offer more attractive contracts than their rules allowed wherever we felt the risk could be safely underwritten.*
>
> c. *Offer to a few named cases a single premium group annuity contract to cover past service of employees, the premium to be figured on 2½% interest as against the 2% rates used by our competitors.*
>
> d. *Make use of Walt's Blue Cross experience to bring out more attractive hospital surgical contracts at lower rates than Association companies. This attracted much attention in the field and caused a split in the Group Association as companies differed on how best to meet our unorthodox offerings. The publicity given us was far greater than we expected in view of the small volume of business we actually wrote.*
>
> e. *Seek most group business from brokers and agents of other companies. The Bankers Life had few city agents and most were not large writers.*

To this outline of operational procedures, Warters might have added that Bankers Life was quite content initially to concentrate on small companies with a minimum of twenty-five employees, companies so small as not to attract the interest of the giants in the field. By concentrating its efforts in the Midwest, in small towns where employees were well known by their employers and their neighbors, Bankers Life could write many contracts with flexible provisions and highly competitive rates which would not have been possible with large companies employing hundreds of anonymous workers.

Bankers Life wrote its first group policy, a health insurance contract, on June 15, 1941, for the Utica Department Store in downtown Des Moines. One month later, it wrote its first pension plan for the Central National Bank, also of Des Moines. By the end of the year, the small home office staff was working sixty to seventy hours a week to handle the number of contracts that were coming in. Art Roberts would remember that in one month alone they had thirty pension plans to process. Warters told them he expected them to do a pension plan a day, and by working nights and weekends, they got the job done. Even so, some business had to be turned down simply because there wasn't the office personnel available to develop the contracts, for unlike ordinary life, there was no standardized policy. Each group plan had to be tailor-made to meet the specific needs of each individual company. Bankers Life, according to Warters, "soon became known as the company willing to issue any contract which could be soundly underwritten [and] willing to tailor the contract to fit the needs of the customer rather than force him into a ready-made suit complying with Association rules." Because of its decision not to join the Group Association and to operate outside its rules, Bankers Life also became known among the old established giants in the field—Metropolitan, Equitable of New York, Travelers, and Aetna—as that pesky little freebooter, willing to move in on business that they had not deemed worthy of consideration and making a considerable amount of money and fame for itself by so doing.

America's abrupt forced entry into World War II in December 1941 created major problems for the company, largely in respect to obtaining and holding trained personnel, both in the home office and out in the field, but paradoxically, the war also proved to be a major contributing factor to Bankers Life's initial success in the group insurance field. With rigid economic controls in effect for the duration, companies could no longer offer wage increases as an incentive for greater production, nor could labor unions demand them in negotiating new contracts. What companies could offer and what unions did demand, however, were greater fringe benefits in the form of pension plans and hospital, health, and accident insurance. Consequently, the years 1941–45 saw a rapid increase throughout the insurance industry in the number of group contracts. This wartime development was officially recognized by the federal government in the 1947 Taft-Hartley Act by allowing such fringe benefits to be a recognized part of collective bargaining along with wages, hours, and union recognition. The official acceptance of group insurance proved to be of tremendous benefit to all companies engaged in that business. Congress also came to the aid of the group insurance companies by passing a law in 1942 allowing company contributions to a pension plan to be written off as a tax deduction. Thus were incentives provided by Washington to both labor and management for the establishment of group insurance contracts. Bankers Life could not have had a more favorable climate into which to enter the group insurance field.

Of particular benefit to Bankers Life in these years was its development of a group permanent program, which when it first appeared was unique in the field. The inspiration for this development came early in 1942, when Bankers Life's New York agency manager, Chet Falkenhainer, took Warters to see an important insurance broker in the city, Ralph Lathrop. Lathrop told Warters that he had a major client, the Sperry Rand Corporation, which was interested in some kind of group insurance on a permanent plan, such as life paid up at sixty-five. There was at that time no such thing as group permanent insurance. Group life provided term insurance coverage for the individual employee only while he was employed by the company. Since he had received this insurance as part of his employment contract on a group basis, without having to take any medical examination, he had no individual claim on the continuity of that insurance. Upon termination of his employment by either resignation or discharge, the life insurance provided by the company was also terminated. The individual, under most state laws, had the opportunity to convert his group life into an individual life policy, but this had to be done upon his initiative and at his expense. The concept of a group permanent program was regarded by most actuaries to be as impossible and impractical of achievement as trying to square the circle or flying to the moon.

Warters, however, did not dismiss Lathrop's request outright. He was intrigued by the idea. Returning to Des Moines, with the assistance of Bill Rae and Earl Bucknell, he went to work on a group permanent plan that would meet state requirements on group insurance, would be attractive to both employer and employee, and would not present an undue risk to Bankers Life. It is a mark of Warters' actuarial genius that he was able to develop a group permanent program that met all of these demands. On November 10, 1942, to the utter astonishment of the industry, Bankers Life announced to all of its agency managers:

> *A new series of policies in the Group Department meeting the need for permanent forms of insurance under Group contracts. These new policies will answer the demand for a form of Group Insurance combining the economies and flexibilitiy obtainable only under a Group contract with the advantages of individual policies written under a Pension Trust.... The new plan will be sold only in the Group Department, using Group underwriting rules and requirements. The Company will not consider any group of less than fifty lives or where less than $250,000 face amount of insurance is involved. The employer is required to pay at least 25% of the cost of the insurance. If employees contribute, at least 75% of those eligible must apply before the insurance can be made effective. The contracts are offered on either a contributory or non-contributory basis, with vesting privileges to meet the employer's wishes.*

It took all of Warters' persuasive powers and his absolute confidence, based upon sound statistical analysis, in the feasibility of the plan to convince state insurance commissions that they should approve of anything as radically innovative as group permanent. Fortunately both Iowa and New York accepted the program late in 1942, and other major states, Ohio, Illinois, and Pennsylvania, followed within a year or two. Although Sperry Rand, whose initial inquiry had set the whole idea in motion, did not buy the program, Marshall Field of Chicago did early in 1943, which, as Warters observed, "gave us a name case of enormous prestige." Other major concerns followed: Daytons' Department Store in Minneapolis, the Outboard Marine Motor Company, the Carrier Air Conditioning Corporation, and the *Chicago Tribune*. With these prestigious companies under group permanent contracts, Bankers Life was no longer exclusively engaged in "baby" group contracts with small companies. It had broken into the big time.

The large insurance companies who had viewed the development of group permanent with utter consternation, being convinced by their actuaries that group permanent would bankrupt Bankers Life and bring discredit on the entire industry, could now no longer scornfully dismiss this development. To be competitive, they were forced against their will to offer group permanent contracts of their own. Bankers Life had tried to keep the details of its contracts as to how it had met the various problems related to individual conversion upon retirement and to state regulations a carefully guarded trade secret, but, of course, this proved to be impossible with so many people outside of the company involved. Soon the giants in the group insurance field were offering group permanent contracts that bore a striking similarity to those of Bankers Life. Some companies did not even attempt to disguise their imitation, copying Bankers Life forms word for word. One large eastern company, in its haste to enter the field, in a couple of instances even forgot to change the name of the carrier, and its first forms contained the name of Bankers Life as the insuring agency in the text of the contract. Bankers Life could at least take pride in the fact that emulation is the highest form of flattery.

The success of the group permanent idea in the mid-1940s had precipitously boosted Bankers Life into prominence within the group insurance field. Although it was still not one of the giants in terms of either premium income or the amount of group insurance in force, it had suddenly become a dangerous competitor to Aetna and Travelers because of its daring innovations. Much of this early success of group permanent is attributable to the fact that it arrived on the scene at precisely the right time in history. As Art Roberts, who was involved in the group department from its very inception, and Bill Schneider, the present senior vice-president for group insurance, have pointed out, group permanent won immediate acceptance from both employer and employee in the mid-1940s because at that moment the economy was rigidly controlled through wage and price freezes. Group permanent filled a void that had existed since the failure of the old group annuity plans during the Depression of the thirties when most companies involved in the selling of group insurance had had to abandon group annuities because they could no longer afford to guarantee fixed annuity payments at a time when interest rates were falling and the real purchasing power of the dollar was rising. But now during the war years and immediately afterward, with the economy rigidly controlled, there was neither inflation nor deflation. A guaranteed retirement income was a true guarantee of real value for pension dollars received. Both the insurance company writing the contract and their clients knew where they stood.

The heyday of group permanent was short-lived, however. Once the controls were lifted in the late 1940s, and in a postwar boom of a rising economy and an ever-upward spiraling inflation, group permanent was not flexible enough to allow for decreasing value of the dollar to satisfy the customers. Group annuities once again came back into popularity, and today group permanent is largely a dead issue. But, for Bankers Life, group permanent's initial success had been sufficiently great and had lasted long enough for the company to become firmly established within the group insurance field.

Bankers Life also benefited greatly by having the courage and good sense to adopt another idea in the group insurance field that came to it from an outside source. Jack Archibald, who was later to become senior vice-president of Bankers Life but who in the 1940s was underwriting vice-president with the responsibility for underwriting all of the company's products, recalls in a memorandum he wrote for the *History of the Group Department* in the company's archives that in 1947, Pat Rogers, an insurance broker from Marshall, Minnesota, contacted Bankers Life with a novel idea for extending group insurance coverage to the small businessman who had only four or five employees. Rogers knew that Bankers Life had a reputation for considering any group insurance proposal no matter how daring, if the risks were acceptable and the proposal could meet state regulatory standards. Rogers in 1947 had formed the Upper Midwest Employers Association so that small employers, by uniting, could obtain benefit plans for their employees which would enable the employers to meet the competitive job offers of larger companies. As Archibald tells the story:

> *Pat realized there were problems in writing insurance on small groups where no evidence of insurability was obtained. He did his own field underwriting and refused to take cases where the average age was high or where there were known impaired risks. He was insistent that if we wrote the coverage we had to reflect the experience under this particular case to the members.*
>
> *In Minnesota, there was no group law and Pat was able to convince Commissioner Harris that writing group insurance through the Upper Midwest Employers Association was*

in the public interest. In April, 1948, Bankers Life entered into a contract of group life and health insurance for members of the Upper Midwest Employers Association. We worked out a special rate basis and a special commission agreement for this case.... Coverage under the Upper Midwest Employers Association was extended to the states of North and South Dakota, Montana and for a while was available in the state of Wisconsin.

When the plan was introduced into Iowa, the Independent Employers Association was formed and the coverage was written in much the same manner, with a trustee of this association as the policyholder rather than the Upper Midwest Employers Association. This idea was used in the states of Iowa, Nebraska, Kansas, Missouri, and Wisconsin after the original idea was disapproved there.

The success of the Upper Midwest Employers Association in offering the advantages of group insurance contracts to the small businessman with only five or six employees attracted considerable attention not only in the small towns but also among the farmers of Minnesota and the Dakotas. If a garage mechanic working in Joe's U-Wreck 'Em, We Fix 'Em Auto Body Shop in Crossroads, Minnesota, could get group health insurance, why shouldn't Farmer Brown and his hired hand, Elmer, get the same advantage of group protection. So reasoned Joseph Thornton, the man in charge of the insurance operations for the entire First National Bank chain in Minnesota. Thornton came to Pat Rogers with the proposal that his rural banks would be willing to serve as the agency to provide their farmer depositors with group insurance coverage without medical examinations if an underwriter could be found who would provide such insurance at a reasonable rate. Rogers at once turned to Bankers Life. The proposal had a strong appeal to the officers of the company, for Bankers Life had always had a commitment to the farmers of the Midwest. "After much discussion," Archibald relates, "we finally offered to write a bank depositor plan and make the depositors associate members of the Upper Midwest Employers Association. This Contract No. 1495 became effective November 1, 1952. The first bank to be insured under the plan was the First National Bank in Marshall, Minnesota.... The depositor plan was very successful in having many members of the First National Bank chain become insured under this plan."

History had gone full cycle. As it had in the beginning, nearly seventy-five years earlier, Bankers Life was once again working directly through small rural banks to insure midwestern farmers, although this time it was on a group rather than an individual basis.

Archibald was not overstating the case when he said the depositor plan "was very successful." In 1978, of the over $100 million of health insurance in force with Bankers Life through Pat Rogers and Old Northwest Company, about $50 million is in the bank depositor plan and a similar amount is on the small employer plan. At about the same time that Rogers and Thornton worked out the depositor plan with Bankers Life in 1952, Rogers and Thornton's son-in-law, Bob Tyson, formed a partnership for marketing both of these products.

Bjorn, in spite of the difficulty of finding personnel in time of war, had built up a small but effective field and home office force within the first two years of his joining Bankers Life: George Lewis, his first appointment, whom he had known at Connecticut General and whom he placed in Houston, Texas; Frank Casey, also from Connecticut General, who worked with Bjorn in the home office; Ed Optekar from Equitable of New York, who served first as the New York group manager and later transferred to Pittsburgh; Henry Morris, who headed up the Chicago office initially; Tom Moore, who soon took over the Chicago office and later established the Milwaukee office; Gren Vale of Prudential, who replaced Optekar in New York; Tom Rainey from General American, who worked in the Los Angeles group office; and Phil Berthiaume, formerly of Travelers, who headed up first the San Francisco and later the Portland, Oregon, office. As Archibald would later observe: "All of these men were topnotch sales people and some of them were not easy to manage. However, the company will always be indebted to them for the efforts which they put forth for the company in those early days."

By 1944, with the success of group permanent, it was apparent that Bankers Life was not only going to survive in the group insurance field but was well on its way to becoming a leader in the group area. Bjorn might well have taken time out to relax and congratulate himself, but he was a man who thrived on challenge. Once the challenge had been met and successfully dealt with, he again grew restless. In July 1944, much to the company's regret, Bjorn resigned to become an independent broker in New York City. In this capacity, he remained a close friend of Bankers Life, directing important clients in its direction. As Warters was to say in his history: "Bankers Life owes much to Walt Bjorn, as without his background experience, his enthusiasm, his friends among the brokers and group sales representatives and his willingness to spend time in travel, our growth would have been much slower and more difficult."

Bjorn left behind a strong field force and men in the home office who were now trained to deal with the management of group insurance: Roberts, Rae, and Archibald. A tradition of strength within the group department had been established which has been maintained over the intervening years with such men as Wendell Moats, Lambert Trowbridge, John Taylor, Robert Larson, Donald Carter, David Hurd, Donald Krieg, Kenneth Barrows, Charles Farr, John Musser, George Fish, and the present senior vice-president who heads up the group division, William Schneider.

By the time Bjorn resigned in 1944, it was already clear that Nollen and the Board had made the right decision to go into group. The future of life insurance in this country to a great extent lay in that field. Schneider and Roberts attribute the amazing growth of group insurance to five major factors: (1) the growing strength of labor unions and the demands they made during the war years and increasingly afterward for such fringe benefits as health insurance and pension plans; (2) the development of separate accounts for pension funds which allowed the investment of these funds in common stock as a hedge against the postwar inflation; (3) the development of a program in 1960 that allowed for the paying of the current interest rate on deposits, instead of the average aggregate interest that the insurance industry had always previously used—called IYI (investment year interest); (4) a federal law of 1959 that allowed the investment income on reserves held by the company under pension plans qualifying under federal law to be tax exempt; and (5) a growing sophistication among insurance companies on how to write flexible, tailor-made contracts that would win wide general acceptance from both management and labor.

Bankers Life by pioneering in such programs as group permanent, small business employers association insurance, the bank depositor plan, and IYI had made a major contribution to the success of group insurance throughout the industry. When Warters had first pushed group insurance in 1940 and Nollen had accepted his recommendations, both men had had the foresight to see that group insurance had the potential to provide a greater stability of income for the company than would be the case if Bankers Life continued to rely solely on individual life and annuity insurance. Neither man in his wildest dreams, however, could have anticipated that within thirty years group insurance would become the overwhelmingly dominant factor in the insurance industry, and particularly so for Bankers Life. By 1978, as the company approached its centennial year, 80 percent of all Bankers Life's premiums received came from group insurance. This statistical fact, which would have astonished Nollen and Warters in 1941 and would have left Jaeger for once in his life speechless, reveals a great deal about the nature not only of insurance in this country but also of our society in general in the late twentieth century. We are increasingly becoming a collectivist society, whether we like it or not—a society in which even those prototypes of rugged individualism, the small-town businessman and the Iowa farmers, find it expedient to form themselves into groups to buy their health insurance.

The entry into the group insurance field was for the Bankers Life Company the dominant concern of the early 1940s. No matter how preoccupied the officers of the company might be with this venture, however, they could hardly ignore the greatest conflict in the history of the world that raged throughout the planet. World War II impinged itself upon every facet of American life for nearly four years and was all-pervasive in everyone's thoughts and actions as the Depression had been a decade before. Although Des Moines was far removed from the battlefields of Europe, Africa, and Asia, and was even a long way from the blacked-out cities and air-raid shelters of America's East and West Coasts, nevertheless the war was total in its societal impact upon Iowa as well. As young men and women left the state by the thousands for military service, as gas rationing restricted travel, as consumer durable goods and construction materials became impossible to obtain, problems related to personnel and daily operational procedures mounted.

Yet, perversely, war also benefited the insurance industry, just as it did those manufacturing plants that could successfully convert themselves into military production. In a period of full employment, people had money to spend but were severely limited as to the consumer products they could buy. Unable to purchase new automobiles, electric refrigerators, or toasters, they turned to insurance not only for protection but as a safe place in which to invest their excess funds. Bankers Life, along with the rest of the industry, profited from these wartime restrictions upon the economy. At the outbreak of the war in Europe in 1939, Bankers Life had $735 million insurance in force—not quite up to the level it had achieved in 1924. Three years later, this figure had increased by $50 million, and by 1945, in the last year of the war, Bankers Life at last broke the $1 billion mark, a goal it had anticipated reaching in 1929. Premium income at $37 million and assets at $364 million were also at an all-time high. All of these figures might have been considerably larger had the company had the personnel available both in the field and in the home office to press the market aggressively.

The impact of the war was reflected in the minutes of every meeting of the Board of Directors during these years. War provisions had to be written in to all new policies issued to males of draft age, jobs had to be guaranteed to those leaving their employment with Bankers Life in order to join the armed services, and salary compensation was provided to those employees on active military service. The gymnasium in the basement of the new home office building was turned over to the Des Moines City Council and Polk County Board of Supervisors as a control center for the Civil Defense Council. Many of the field agents volunteered or were drafted for military service, and those who remained, particularly in the rural areas with a large territory to cover, found it increasingly and frustratingly difficult to get to customers who had the money and the desire to buy insurance. The plight of the sales agent was somewhat ameliorated, however, by the company's providing a group pension plan for the field force effective January 1, 1942. This was extended to all agency office clerical staffs on April 1, 1942, and the home office plan was revised to provide hospital and surgical benefits on July 1, 1942.

The war also greatly affected the company's investment policy, further accentuating a policy begun during the Depression of investing heavily in government bonds. In the 1930s, this had been done in order to have a greater liquidity of assets. Now in an all-out war, governmental pressure and social responsibility resulted in the company's increasing its holdings in government securities from $67 million in 1941 to $196 million in 1945. Because of the exceedingly high price that municipal bonds brought in these years, President Nollen and the Finance Committee, as Nollen later said, "took advantage of the profits available on the sale of such bonds and reinvested the proceeds in governments." Such exchanges, Nollen further explained:

> *Could be made in an advantageous basis largely because the Federal Government had accentuated its cheap-money policy*

for the war period, reducing interest rates on investments to an even lower figure than that existing prior to the war. The Government's interest pattern provided for a maximum rate of 2½ percent on long-time Government issues. This cheap-money policy of the Government influenced the interest rate of all investments and, accordingly, forced a decline in the interest realized by all life insurance companies on their invested funds. The declining rate of interest earned by life insurance companies on their investments produced a problem entirely new to the life insurance business. Never before had a situation arisen under which the current rate of interest earned by many companies was reduced to a figure below the return guaranteed on outstanding policy contracts. The Bankers Life, in common with other leading life insurance companies of the country, had old business on its book carrying a guaranteed interest rate of 3½ percent, while the current earning rate was finally reduced to a shade under 3 percent. The Bankers Life Company met this situation by applying all profits on the sale of securities and a portion of the Company's current surplus earnings as extra additions to the regular policy reserve funds. The reserves were strengthened to meet future contract obligations based on a continued rate of interest earning at current low levels.

The fiscal policies of the federal government as developed during the previous twelve years of depression and war and Bankers Life's response were reflected in the comparative shifts in the distribution of assets between 1941 and 1945. As mentioned above, the investment in U. S. Government securities rose from $67 million to $195 million, while the amount invested in state and municipal bonds shrank from $40 million to $14 million. Industrial bonds held by the company nearly doubled, from $3.66 million to $6.5 million, and because of a change in the Iowa investment laws and the favorable rate of return, the company had a small investment—$607,000—in preferred stock. First mortgage loans on farm property dropped from $34 million to $28 million, while the figures on first mortgage loans on city property were nearly the reverse, increasing from $25.5 million to $38 million. With wartime prosperity and a shortage of consumer goods, there was a marked decrease in policy loans, from $36.33 million in 1941 down to $24 million in 1945. And in conformity to the deliberate policy of the company to increase its surplus

In 1938 visiting agents stand around the foundation of the future home office.

When the 711 High Street home office was being built in 1938 and 1939,
The Bankers Life provided a "Kibitzers' Gallery" for interested passersby
to safely stop and peek at the progress.

711 High: The original structure of the present home office building was
recognized by Architectural Record as "The Building of the Decade" for
its economical and efficient solutions to the problems affecting all
commercial buildings. Since that time the original building has been
expanded with six additions.

Some Highlights in Tour Of Bankers Life Building

The 550 home office employes of the Bankers Life Co. here went to work Mar. 25 in their new $2,000,000 building, pictures of which are shown in this special photogravure section.

In its new seven-story structure, the Bankers Life Co. sought to construct a modern, efficient life insurance plant. Many of the office, laboratory, personnel, lighting and ventilating features designed toward this end are pictured on this page.

Some of the other features of the building attracting wide comment include the precipitron filter which clears all smoke and dust particles from the air; ventilated individual coat racks, enclosed by rolling shutter doors; transferable steel walls; perforated steel ceilings providing for air conditioning; copper tubes carrying hot or cold water through exterior walls to offset exterior weather conditions; master thermostats to adjust interior temperatures automatically to meet changing conditions outside; teakwood-paneled directors' room of floating, radio-station type of construction; and the concealed wiring of electric, buzzer and telephone systems.

The building is expected to be open for public inspection for four days starting Tuesday.

Areas 53 Feet Wide and 234 feet long are constructed without columns to give the new Bankers Life building great open office areas. Girders, which make this possible, are covered with metal covers. More than a thousand four-foot square light coffers provide diffused light of 32 footcandles at each desk top. The metal, soundproof ceiling is light ivory. Even air distribution is provided through ceiling perforations.

Another Office View shows the enameled steel walls which are interchangeable. They are green to provide a soft, cool working atmosphere.

Rows of Oak Bookcases are built into the legal library on the sixth floor. This room is 22x39 feet.

Looking Up at the High st. entrance, the new Bankers Life structure presents this view. The building is faced with 10,600 cubic feet of Rainbow granite from Cold Springs, Minn., and 30,000 cubic feet of Ileo cream vein limestone from Bedford, Ind. Directly over the bronze-fitted entrance, the art of molded glass panels presents American Indian lore. Casement windows above are set in large panels of glass brick.

(Kodiak Blessing Photo)

From the Photostat Room on the third floor of the new building, Bankers Life employes can obtain a complete photostat of an insurance application in eight minutes. The 17x36-foot room has enameled steel walls, rubber floor and a Dutch door. Muriel Hougen (left) and Helen Holt inspect the photostat equipment above.

Featured on the Main Floor of the new building is this auditorium with seats for 1,200 persons. The main floor is 65x84 feet and the room is 21 feet high. Plaster light coffers in the gold acoustic ceiling combine lighting and ventilation with an aircoustical directing incoming air through the fixture. Single chairs are stored under the stage and all seats can be removed so the floor may be used as a basketball court. A built-in loud speaker at the top of the stage may be tuned in to radio programs. Another speaker directly back of the screen provides sound for films. The auditorium is equipped with projection booth, two film projection machines and a talkie slide projector. Tan rubber wainscoting protects the walls. Two dressing rooms and a check room are provided.

Floy Anderson, Bankers Life laboratory technician, had an active part in designing the third floor medical laboratory in which she is shown above. The laboratory, used for tests in connection with insurance policy applications, includes acid-proof sinks of alberene stone and foot-operated faucets. Near it are three doctors' offices and a dental unit. The medical sector also includes a men's hospital with three beds and a women's hospital which will accommodate eight.

A page from the special Sunday supplement run by the Des Moines Register *when the home office building opened its doors in 1940.*

GLASS BLOCK
CREAM VEIN BEDFORD LIMESTONE
BRONZE WINDOW FRAME
BRONZE HOOD
LIGHT REFLECTORS IN BRONZE HOOD
MOULDED GLASS PANELS
RAINBOW GRANITE
BRONZE LETTERS
CAST BRONZE ORNAMENT
BRONZE DOORS
RAINBOW GRANITE STEPS

BANKERS LIFE COMPANY

FOUNDED 1879

The inviting front entrance to the home office has always been a favorite place for a breath of fresh air or noon lunches. Above the brass doors are three molded glass panels, the work of two midwestern artists, Lowell Houser and Glenn Chamberlain. They depict the colorful myths and picturesque lore of the American Indian, original inhabitants of the land at the fork of the Des Moines and Raccoon rivers, where Des Moines stands today.

Long before physical fitness became a primary concern of both young and old, the company's gym received ample workout during lunch hours and after work. Today, company basketball, volleyball, softball, and bowling teams compete on a city-wide basis.

One of the attractions of the home office building when it was first opened in 1940 was the open viewing area of the building's air conditioning system. The home office was the first office building in Des Moines to be completely air conditioned.

The new home office boasted not only some of the most modern architecture of its time, but also some of the most modern equipment, like this 1940 photostat machine that could produce copies of reports and papers in eight seconds.

Atop the former auditorium entrance rose a granite etching that symbolized Iowa's historical background. The etching was removed in 1976 to make room for another addition to the building.

Before the additions to the home office were built, the third floor sun deck was a favorite spot for lunch.

Located across the street from the main home office building, the annex is connected by an underground tunnel and a skywalk.

Nollen Plaza will be the outdoor park and performance area where the Civic Center of Greater Des Moines will present free concerts, plays, and other events. The Bankers Life suggested the name in recognition of the Nollen family, influential leaders of central Iowa's commercial and educational development. Gerard and Henry Nollen played significant roles in the development of The Bankers Life and of the insurance industry.

Ping-Pong was a popular pastime during the 1930s and 1940s. Former President Gerard Nollen observes the tournament play in the background.

Basketball teams like this early 1940 one competed in city tournaments.

Celebrating at the company's 75th Anniversary dinner, 1954.

A "Bankers Life talent" captured his audience with his act during an early 1940s Christmas party. In top hat and tux, Bill Rae, former vice-president, emceed the affair.

These field group representatives visited the home office in 1945 to improve their technical expertise and presentation skills. Front Row: Dennis Warters, Tom Moore, Gerard Nollen, Phil Berthiaume, Jack Archibald. Second Row: Tom Rainey, Charles DeWinter, George Matheson, Ed Optekar, Gordon Randall, Georg Fish, Henry Morris. Third Row: Art Roberts, Charles Southern, George Lewis, Don Hopkins, George Bailey, Bill Rae, Frank Casey.

To recognize the company's outstanding agents whose dedication to policyowners and service has qualified them for membership in the company's Top Honor Clubs 20 times or more, Merv Cramer, retired senior vice-president and member of the Board of Directors, dedicated the Hall of Fame in the home office in 1972.

Key men at The Bankers Life early in the new century. From left: I. M. Earle, general counsel; Henry S. Nollen, secretary; E. E. Clark, vice-president; Simon Casady, treasurer; Edward A. Temple, president; Dr. F. J. Will, medical director; George Kuhns, field manager.

Four presidents of The Bankers Life: Gerard Nollen (1926-1946), Earl Bucknell (1961-1974), Edmund M. McConney (1946-1956), Dennis N. Warters (1956-1961).

Presidents of The Bankers Life

Edward A. Temple, 1879

E. E. Clark, 1909

George Kuhns, 1916

Gerard S. Nollen, 1926

Edmund M. McConney, 1946

D. N. Warters, 1956

E. F. Bucknell, 1961

Harold G. Allen, 1968

Robert N. Houser, 1973

The Bankers Life Board of Directors, as of annual meeting 1979

Harold G. Allen
Retired Chairman of the
Board and Chief Executive
Officer, The Bankers Life

Howard R. Bowen
R. Stanton Avery Professor
of Economics and
Education, Claremont
Graduate School

William J. Goodwin, Jr.
President, Goodwin
Companies

Robert N. Houser
President and
Chief Executive Officer,
The Bankers'Life

Downing B. Jenks
Chairman and Chief
Executive Officer, Missouri
Pacific Corporation and
Chairman of the Missouri
Pacific Railroad Company

Thomas S. Nurnberger
Formerly Executive Vice-
President, American
Telephone and Telegraph

J. Louis Robertson
Retired Vice-Chairman of
the Board of Governors,
Federal Reserve System
Director of Temporary
Investment Fund, Inc.

Lyle C. Roll
Chairman Emeritus of the
Board of the Kellogg
Company

William G. Schneider
Senior Vice-President,
The Bankers Life

Fred M. Seed
Retired President,
Cargill, Inc.

Dwight H. Swanson
President and Chairman
of the Board, Iowa Power
and Light Company

John R. Taylor
Executive Vice-President,
The Bankers Life

Darwin Tucker
Retired Corporate
President and Chief
Operating Officer,
National Gypsum
Company

L. Emmerson Ward
Chairman, Board of
Development,
Mayo Foundation

David E. Babcock
Chairman of the Board
and Chief Executive
Officer, May Department
Stores Company

Fred W. Weitz
Chief Executive Officer,
President and Chairman
of the Board,
Weitz Brothers, Inc.

in order to meet its contract obligations as mentioned above by Nollen, surplus funds were increased from $15.8 million to $21.7 million, an increase of 37 percent as a protective hedge against the drop in the rate of interest earned on invested funds over the past four years from 3.64 to 3.03 percent. Born out of an emergency situation of depression followed by war, these investment policies nevertheless established new patterns which were to prevail in the postwar decades.

On September 1, 1945, on the battleship *Missouri*, the Japanese envoys signed the documents of surrender, and the greatest war in world history was over. Alone among the great powers, the United States emerged from this war physically intact, its land unravaged by invading troops, its cities untouched by aerial bombardment. The task of rebuilding a shattered planet was as staggering in its immensity as the job of destroying had been, and much of the burden of reconstruction of necessity had to be borne by the United States. At the same time, its own citizens, deprived for four years of those consumer goods they regarded as basic to the American way of life, were eagerly lining up for the sweet fruits of peace: new automobiles, refrigerators, washing machines, and Levittown houses. There was, consequently, no postwar economic slump in 1947–48 as there had been in 1920–21. Even with 13 million ex-G.I.'s returning to the labor market, there was no shortage of jobs. America was entering a new era of a rapidly expanding economy, and the Depression now seemed as remote in time as the Middle Ages.

The Bankers Life Company entered this era of postwar prosperity and expansion with new administrative leadership. Gerard Nollen, who had been president for twenty years, during two of the most tumultuous decades in American history, and now having already passed the normal retirement age, decided it was an appropriate moment to step down. Early in 1946 he announced his retirement, effective at the annual meeting in April 1946. But the company was unwilling to sever all connections with the most effective president it had had during its nearly three quarters of a century of existence. Instead, the Board asked Nollen not to step down but rather to step up to a new position, created for him, that of Chairman of the Board.

There was no question as to who would be Nollen's successor as president of the company. For the past ten years it had been obvious to all that Edmund McConney was the heir apparent, and immediately following Nollen's resignation in April the Board unanimously elected McConney president.

To this office, McConney brought very real strength. Born in 1891 on the island of St. Christopher in the British West Indies, where his father served as Episcopal rector, McConney after graduating from Harrison College in the Barbados at the age of nineteen had migrated to Toronto, Canada, where he became a clerk in a Canadian insurance company, Manufacturers Life. In 1914 he enlisted in the Canadian infantry, serving for four years on the front lines in France only to be severely wounded on the last night of the war, November 10, 1918. While spending several months in the hospital, he completed his studies to become an actuary and upon his discharge from the hospital, passed the actuarial examinations and became an associate of the British Institute of Actuaries. In September 1919 he came to Des Moines to accept a position in the actuarial department of Bankers Life. Within a few months after his arrival, he was elected assistant actuary and four years later, became the chief actuary of the company. Nollen soon after becoming president in 1926 began grooming McConney for high office by giving him responsibilities outside of the actuarial department both in the agency field and on the Investment Committee.

McConney had all of the Gaelic wit and charm, with none of the grim dourness, of his Scottish ancestry. A brilliant raconteur, McConney was probably the most effective public speaker of all the officers in the company, a man who could charm any audience with his unlimited supply of anecdotes and jokes, many of them being directed against himself and his Scottish heritage. Immensely popular both within and outside the company, McConney became a prominent figure within the life insurance industry long before he became president of Bankers Life. He was chosen by the industry to be a member of the Agents Compensation Committee of the Life Insurance Sales Research Bureau, and served as chairman of that committee for three years. The report that this committee made in 1943 resulted in the modernization of agency contracts throughout the life insurance field.

McConney was also active in both of the professional actuarial societies that then existed in the United States, the Actuarial Society of America and the American Institute of Actuaries. He was an early advocate of joining these two societies into one organization, and when this was finally accomplished in 1948, McConney's efforts were recognized by his election as first president of the newly fused Society of Actuaries.

The transition from Nollen to McConney was not abrupt or as markedly different as that which had occurred when Nollen succeeded Kuhns in the presidency. Although no one could hope to duplicate Nollen's role in the company, McConney's interests were essentially the same as Nollen's. The two men's early careers within the company were remarkably similar. Both were adaptive to changing conditions, receptive to new ideas, basically conservative in philosophy yet progressive in outlook. If McConney lacked Nollen's Olympian prestige within the company, he was more easily approachable, more relaxed and affable in his daily dealings with his staff and the general public. Under McConney, the basic policies as established by Nollen during years of depression and war would be developed and enlarged in the postwar period but would remain essentially the same.

There were other significant changes in top management in these immediate postwar years in addition to the change in the presidency. Bert Mills, for reasons of health, retired in 1946 and was succeeded as secretary of the company by J. S. Corley. Bill Jaeger, who had never become reconciled to the decision to enter the group insurance field, retired as senior vice-president in April 1942, but remained active within the company as vice-chairman of the Board. Jaeger's successor to the office of agency vice-president was Bill Winterble, and Dwight Brooke succeeded Joe Lorentzen as general counsel in 1947. Young men were moving to the forefront in these years of transition: John Archibald as underwriting vice-president, Earl Bucknell, vice-president and actuary, Marvin Lewis as director of agencies, John Grimes as agency secretary, and Bob Patrick as financial vice-president. The old order, of necessity, was changing, but the transition to the new order was neither revolutionary nor disruptive. "Onward" the company's field journal proudly proclaimed in its title, and "Upward" the annual reports clearly showed.

With each passing year, group insurance became an ever larger factor in the company's sales records. In 1952 the decision was made to enter the individual accident and health insurance field. The overall responsibility for planning the entry into this field was assigned to Jack Archibald, in addition to his other responsibilities, and he recruited Harry Graham to manage the nonsales aspects of the new department.

The summer of 1954 marked the seventy-fifth year of the company's existence, which the company duly celebrated with a "Big

Show Party" at the KRNT Theater and a Diamond Jubilee dinner dance at the Hotel Savery. Even more satisfying than the planned celebrations were the figures that could be stated in the annual report: Insurance in force for the first time passed the $2 billion mark—it had taken sixty-six years to reach the first billion-dollar goal, only nine years to pass the second billion-dollar mark. Assets were now up to the $750 million level, and annual premium income was over $84 million. This growth was reflected in the crowded office space in the home office on High Street. After only fourteen years of occupancy, it was already time to start plans for the expansion of the building. Mr. Temple's once "quiet, insignificant little child" was clearly no longer either insignificant or little.

6/Mr. Temple's Child Becomes a Giant

1954-1979

Two years after Bankers Life celebrated its seventy-fifth birthday, Edmund McConney retired from the presidency of the company he had served for nearly half of its existence. In retirement he could take pride in the fact that during the ten years he had served as chief executive, he had successfully maintained the basic policies of the Nollen administration. Under his leadership, the company had made a smooth transition from wartime strictures to peacetime expansion. The fact that the United States had become involved in another major conflict in the Far East during a part of the past decade had had little effect upon either the operating procedures or the achievements of the company as measured by sales and assets. McConney could turn the company over to new leadership with considerable personal satisfaction.

McConney was succeeded to the presidency on October 29, 1956, by Dennis Warters. Joining the company in 1920 at the age of twenty-three, only one year after McConney had entered the employ of Bankers Life, Warters had closely followed his predecessor up each rung of the same ladder from actuarial assistant to president. Like McConney, he was born a British subject, had emigrated to Canada and had received his education there. Similar as the two men were in antecedents and experience, McConney and Warters were poles apart in disposition, as far distant in temperament as were the places of their birth, the British West Indies and Birmingham, England. Just as the congenial warmth of his birthplace on St. Christopher Island had become an integral part of McConney's personality, so it seemed had the cold, gray austerity of England's Midlands left its initial scar on Warters. Warters would never achieve the affectionate regard of the agents as had Kuhns, nor the almost reverential respect that was paid to Nollen, nor the easy camaraderie that McConney had established with the entire Bankers Life family. By disposition reserved, perhaps even somewhat shy in personal relationships, Warters was perforce destined to live behind the high walls of associational isolation which his own nature had built around him. Yet if he would never win a popularity contest among the executive officers of the company, he could carry off top honors for intelligence and creativity. No one in the history of the company had surpassed him in imaginative originality or in the ability to test his own highly innovative ideas with the cold, objective analysis of a logician or a physical scientist.

In respect to management, he was, like Kuhns, a man of strong will who did not take easily any criticism of his policies, other than that which he himself offered. And like Nollen, he did not suffer fools gladly. Warters was a strong, forceful chief executive, but many of his fellow officers felt that he often kept them in the dark as to his own position in regard to the issue at hand until after a decision had been made by them. He was then frequently far too abrasive in public toward those subordinates who had, in his opinion, made the wrong decision. His frequent "second-guessing" of those responsible for various operations caused a tension within the company that had not existed under either Nollen or McConney.

Warters, however, could be a shrewd judge of men who would best serve the company. His immediate successor, Earl Bucknell, would later praise Warters for this ability to pick the right men for the right jobs. Bucknell offered as illustration, two key appointments that Warters made soon after becoming president in 1956. The first was his choice of Jack Archibald to head up the group department. No other department in the company was more central to Warters' interest than was this department. It had been Warters who initially re-searched this insurance field for Bankers Life. It had been the logic of his irrefutable arguments that had convinced Nollen to make the big decision to go into group insurance in spite of the very powerful opposition to the idea within the company. And it had been the success of group insurance that firmly established Warters' prestige within the company and had made him the logical successor to McConney. Warters might well have elected to hold firmly to the group department as his own special province, but instead he made a strong appointment and then gave to Jack Archibald the authority to run his own show, which the latter did superbly well.

Another major personnel decision of Warters was to bring Merv Cramer in from the field to head up the ordinary sales department. Again, Warters had not allowed his own predilection for group insurance to blind him to the continuing importance of individual life. And in Cramer, who had made the Los Angeles agency a sales leader in the field, Warters had once again chosen precisely the right man for the right job. As Bucknell succinctly points out, Cramer was "bright, a tireless worker, a man with a dynamic personality who had come up through every layer of the Ordinary field operations," and a man, like Jaeger, who "was immediately accepted by the fieldmen as one of their own." It should be remembered that Cramer had been one of the first of the field agents to accept the idea of group insurance, and it had been he whom Nollen had called upon to speak for group insurance at the sales convention in which it was announced that Bankers Life would enter the group insurance field. Cramer was not afraid of new ideas and new methods. A staunch supporter of the fieldmen of whom he had so recently been a part, Cramer nevertheless could at the same time realize that increasingly the selling of insurance, both group and individual, would be dependent upon insurance brokers. Cramer envisioned for Bankers Life a growth in sales so great as to necessitate a full exploitation of both the traditional field agencies and the new—at least for Bankers Life—brokerage firms.

Cramer, who had with considerable reluctance finally yielded to Warters' importuning, came to the home office in 1959 as director of agencies to succeed Bob Shay, who had died the previous year. Working under Marvin Lewis, successor to Bill Winterble as agency vice-president, Cramer immediately gave a new life and sparkle to the entire marketing operations of individual life and health insurance. During the fifteen years he was to serve in the home office as director of agencies, as field vice-president and then in 1963 as Lewis' successor to the agency vice-presidency and finally in 1970, as senior vice-president in charge of individual life, Cramer, with all of the enthusiasm once shown by Bill Jaeger, stimulated the field agents to greater production records through many innovations. He gave to the agents and managers the opportunity of directly contributing to home office policies by recommending to President Allen the creation in 1971 of the Agents' Advisory Council, for the individual field agents, and the Agency Managers' Marketing Council, as a successor to the old Agency Managers' Advisory Committee created by President Nollen. These two councils had direct access to top management, including the president, and they frequently made forceful suggestions which were later implemented through the adoption of new policies and the creation of new products.

The old means of recognizing top salesmen—annual conventions and top production clubs, first instituted by Kuhns and Nollen—were continued, but Cramer went further than his predecessors by creating a permanent pantheon for the supersalesmen. In 1972, at his recommendation, a Hall of Fame was established for those agents who had managed to qualify for the top production club for twenty or more years. Forty-two agents were admitted into the Hall of Fame upon its creation, and from 1972 through 1978, an additional sixteen agents qualified to join this select company of stars. (For a complete listing of the Hall of Fame members, see the Appendix.) The field agents quite obviously loved these innovations and the man who had designed them.

Cramer also followed through in pushing individual life sales in the brokerage market. He gave Roland Franquemont the responsibility for developing the brokerage business, and under Franquemont's direction the brokerage sales of individual life were to grow from less than 5 percent to over one third of total individual life sales in the next fifteen years.

A similar stimulation in sales was also taking place within the group department in the late 1950s and the 1960s under the able direction of Jack Archibald, with Wendell Moats in charge of the group sales organization, Lambert Trowbridge in charge of group pensions, and Bill Schneider in charge of group life and health. The group department had, from the beginning, developed its own sales organization with a select staff of salaried sales experts who could develop group business through the regular Bankers Life field agents as well as through agents of other companies, brokers, and consultants. Wendell Moats built over the years a large dynamic sales organization. Unlike most group sales organizations, this one was cross-trained in pensions on the one hand and life and health on the other, which greatly added to the strength of the group department and put it in a strong position to increase its share of the pension and profit-sharing market when the tremendous expansion of that market occurred in the 1970s. Moats inaugurated formal training programs which effectively moved the sales organization toward the professionalism so essential to success in the years of rapid expansion. He was responsible for the recruiting and much of the training of most of those field personnel in management positions today. Group sales had its own sales incentive programs, group sales contests, including the Premium Sweepstakes, the Case Derby, and the Performance Pacer, and under Moats developed its own Group Marketing Council.

The experienced group men recruited in the 1950s developed into a corps of aggressive producers in the 1960s. The leaders included Frank Weisman in Chicago, Wes Bray of Detroit and New York, Bob Schroeder in Des Moines, and Joe Nally in Philadelphia, who, with their sales teams, were sporting derbies and red ties, which historically signified group sales contest winners.

When Moats retired in 1970, he was succeeded by Bob Larson, the current vice-president in charge of group sales. Larson brought to the job a wealth of experience in group operations, having previously been the officer in charge of all group life and health divisions. In that capacity, he had displayed an unusual balance between the need for aggressive sales and financial responsibility. His move to the top sales position was somewhat unusual in that he had never been a member of the field organization. However, he was well known and highly regarded by the field personnel who had become well acquainted with his abilities in many sales situations with prospects and customers. Larson provided the technical expertise and imagination in many such situations. Larson succeeded in upgrading the group field organization and building it further. As the sales staff expanded, field sales management skills were sharpened to broaden the effectiveness of the group sales specialists. Many of the younger people were hired untrained and developed rapidly into a new group of leaders. So the corps of the sixties mushroomed into a powerful sales force which began setting new records with their increased productivity.

The natural marketing thrust for a group department is toward the larger employers and bargaining units. Jack Archibald and his associates recognized, however, that the smaller employers needed group products just as much as the larger groups. This market was not getting the attention that the larger groups were. Bankers Life decided that in addition to continuing strong pursuit of the larger employers it should develop products that would be particularly attractive to the smaller employer. It did this in the group life and health area through its Planned Employee Program (PEP) product and in the pension area by extending its product down to smaller sizes and eventually developing prototype plans. Moreover, with the urging of George Fish, who had been active in the development of the Upper Midwest program mentioned earlier, the department sold a number of association-type cases—another device for reaching the small employer. In this way the Bankers' group department was selling and administering plans for groups as small as two or three employees to the very large employers with many thousands of employees—such as Humble Oil and Beatrice Foods.

As Archibald approached retirement age, he turned the group department over to his longtime associate Bill Schneider, who inherited a highly qualified staff which Archibald had built up. Archibald in his long years of service in many different departments had contributed much to the success of Bankers Life, but his bringing cohesion to the sprawling and rapidly growing group department must be regarded as one of his major contributions to the company. The group department was ready to face the challenges of the 1970s— and they were many: volatile interest rates with their impact upon pension pricing, rampant inflation, escalating medical claims, mushrooming regulation of group medical insurance at the state level, and the demands of the Employee Retirement Income Security Act (ERISA) at the federal level.

To meet these challenges, the department had some particularly strong people in key positions not only in the sales organization but also in home office management. In addition to Schneider himself, who provided the real leadership, there was Don Krieg, who was in charge of the group life and health division. Krieg had been instrumental in the development of the group life and health products and technical sales. For the next three years until he was given the new responsibility in 1974 of forming and operating a new property liability company for Bankers Life, Krieg provided strong leadership for the life and health divisions. In charge of the group pension division was Dave Hurd. This department was soon to experience the difficult administrative task of bringing thousands of pension customers into compliance with ERISA regulations at the same time it was undergoing the most explosive growth the department had yet known. No man, fortunately, was more cognizant of the pension industry than he, and as a member and later chairman of the insurance industry's Pension Committee, Hurd was able to keep current with ERISA regulations as they developed. In recognition of his services to both the industry and his own company, he was later to be appointed as the industry's representative on the ERISA Advisory Council to the U.S. Department of Labor.

The rapid growth in group life and health was due in no small part to the company's concern for a humane and nonlegalistic approach to claim payments. Ken Barrows had been in charge of the claim department from 1945 until he became vice-president in charge of Health Care Relations in 1971. During that period, the expanding group health sales led to a rapid expansion of the claim operations under Barrows. The emphasis was upon promptness and understanding for the claimant's point of view. This policy in respect to claims won thousands of friends for the company and was particularly important at a time when all insurance companies were finding it necessary to increase group premium rates to match the rapidly rising cost of health care. Barrows' work was given industry-wide recognition when he was named president of the International Claim Association in 1964.

When Barrows assumed his new position in 1971, he was succeeded by Don Carter, who had early in his career been in the group underwriting area and was later moved to the planning division. Now back in the group area, in charge not only of the group claim division but also the group life and health divisions, Carter was to pursue the same policies that Barrows had established in respect to claims and was to receive the same recognition from the insurance industry when he was designated president-elect of the International Claim Association in the year of Bankers Life's centennial.

As the competition for pension dollars became more sophisticated, it was apparent that greater help would be needed in making an investment-sales approach. Earlier attempts at having investment specialists make joint customer and prospect calls with pension specialists from the group department and group field had proven the value of such combinations. However, the pace was quickening to such an extent that it was clear the group department would have to establish an investment expert and trainer on its own staff. Art Roberts, who had been with the group department from the outset and had experience in administration, in product design, and in account executive work, took this assignment. He worked closely with investment personnel, with group field personnel, and with home office pension personnel to develop educational information and competitive information with respect to investments and to help with particularly important sales situations. This development contributed heavily to Bankers Life's increasing share of the pension market in the 1970s.

Another key figure in the group area during these years of rapid growth was Charles Farr, who had the group actuarial responsibility and had been associated with the group department since the early 1950s.

With this staff, the challenges of the 1970s were to be met. The group department's premium income exploded. In less than a decade, it was to nearly quadruple, from $300 million in 1970 to well over $1 billion by the time of the centennial. Meeting these challenges did not prove to be an easy task for those involved. Growth as rapid as this necessitated a rapid staff expansion, and there was constant pressure for more space and equipment. The home office auditorium, which had been Nollen's particular pride when the building was first designed, as well as some hallways and part of the basement area, had to be sacrificed to work space. But by 1979 it was clear that the group department had truly arrived. Its premium income accounted for some 80 percent of the company's total, and Bankers Life group was now among the eight largest group operations in the country.

This phenomenal growth of Bankers Life group insurance was certainly due in part to the aggressive marketing policies of its sales organization, the effectiveness of its top management, and the innovative planning and development of new products by such key personnel as Warters, Archibald, Bill Rae, Lambert Trowbridge, Bill Schneider, Bob Larson, Dave Hurd, Don Krieg, and Don Carter. Had not Bankers Life pushed aggressively in a field already crowded with such giant insurance companies as Metropolitan, Prudential, and Travelers with new products and new ideas, it would never have had a chance of securing a share of an increasingly important market. Emphasis must be given, however, to the fact that the market was there for those companies aggressive and innovative enough to exploit it. Group insurance was merely one manifestation of a changing social fabric in America in the postwar years. Big business, big labor, and big government had all combined to force a collectivization of society resulting in new demands and expectations unknown in the early decades of the twentieth century. Pensions and other fringe benefits such as health and accident insurance were now major considerations for both business organizations in recruiting new personnel and labor unions in their collective bargaining negotiations with management. The Great Depression and the Social Security Act of 1935 had made people acutely conscious of the need for security in sickness and old age, and the public looked not only to government but also to the private sector for that security. Employee benefits were now as much a part of the conditions for employment as wages and hours of work. Fortunately for Bankers Life, it had both the products and the organization to take advantage of this major social phenomenon.

The annual accumulation of funds that resulted from this growth meant an ever-increasing importance of the investment field to the company. Investment of assets must always be a major consideration for any insurance company. Mutual life companies are not like General Motors or the family-owned corner drugstore. They sell a product, to be sure, but the funds they receive for that product do not belong to a single or small group of company owners or to a large group of corporate stockholders. These funds essentially belong to the company itself as steward for the policyholders, and the price that is paid in premiums for the insurance protection the policyholders receive is strongly affected by how wisely the insurance company invests the premiums that are paid for that protection. Insurance companies, of necessity, must be financial investment houses as surely as any bank or savings and loan association.

Robert Patrick, who during the post–World War II years of rapid growth served as the chief investment officer of the company, has written for the company archives a brief but illuminating history of the Bankers Life Company's investment policies from its beginnings until 1970. Patrick's history emphasizes that Bankers Life had from the start always pursued a policy of sound and conservative investment. Simon Casady served as the senior investment official for over forty years, from 1887 until his death in 1928, and although the company expanded greatly during that period, its basic conservative investment policies remained constant. Nor was there any dramatic change in policy under Casady's successor, George Fowler, who was in charge of the company's investments from 1928 until his retirement in 1944.

If anything, the traumatic experience of the Great Depression in the early 1930s when, as Patrick says in his history, "investment losses became heavy, property values declined precipitously, and the confidence of investors in the policies that had been pursued for years was practically destroyed," made Fowler even more conservative in outlook. "The Company's experience with investments in the 1932–33 depression left a deep mark on him as it did on most investment men of that day." Fowler, like his predecessor, was a man of great personal integrity. Noted for his ability as a golfer, Fowler was paid a high and deserved tribute by one of his associates in the company and on the Wakonda golf course who said, "George's life was like his golf game, right down the middle."

If the stated and practiced policies of the company were essentially conservative in the investment field, this did not mean that the personnel most directly concerned with investment policies were colorless, dull automatons, nourished only by statistics and the financial pages of *Barron's Weekly*. Some of these men were the equal of the most colorful individualists within the entire organization— men like C. C. Dabney, who headed up the company's loan investments in Texas and always dressed the part of a Texas ranger, complete with cowboy boots, broad-brimmed Stetson hat, and gun, or the stern Dutch Methodist from Pella, Iowa, John H. Vanderlinden, who as farm loan inspector in Iowa in the late 1920s could at a glance tell a good farm risk from a bad one with the awful certainty of a John Calvin picking the saints from the sinners. The stories told and retold within the company of Dabney's ability to bedazzle the Texan rancher with his spectacular dress and his exuberant manners and of the ability of his close associate, Bing Wolson, to collect in full on defaulted municipal loans were as numerous and as humorous as any of the many legends built around the activities of some of the company's more colorful sales agents.

Much of the company's success in the farm loan field, which dominated the company's investments until the Depression of the 1930s, was because the company had men in the investment operations who knew land and farmers from actual field experience, men like Dabney, Wolson and E. D. Burchette in Texas, Vanderlinden, Roy McAllister, Frank Charlton, Joe Auner, E.R. Morison and Gerry Rickert in the Upper Midwest, whose judgment the investment officers in the home office, Fowler, L.L. Cassidy, John Corley, Gene McAnelly, H.E. Handford, Blaine Davis, Harle Bishop, and Patrick could rely upon with assurance. Bankers Life was proud of being an Iowa company, and Iowa meant agriculture. Almost from its inception, the Association had served the Iowa farmer in providing him insurance on his life and loans to promote his livelihood. It is hardly surprising, then, that the major outlet for the company's investments should be in farm loans. For the long run, there seemed no better investment than the rich farmlands of Iowa, Minnesota, and the eastern Dakotas. The prosperity of the company was inextricably linked to the successful farming operations of the region it served. As a consequence, the investment department of the company in these years built up one of the ablest farm loan forces in the nation. The annual statements of the company give graphic evidence of the importance of farm real estate to the investment department. In 1911, the last year of the old mutual benefit society's existence, the Association had assets totaling $18,619,181. Of this amount,

$15,631,833, or 84 percent of the total assets of the company, was invested in first mortgage loans, principally in Iowa farm real estate, with a few mortgages on Des Moines city property.

The newly incorporated mutual company, Bankers Life Company, continued the investment policies of the Association. In 1916 the company was authorized by the Iowa insurance commissioner to make farm loans in Texas, Nebraska, Minnesota, and South Dakota, and in the following year, of its $32 million assets, $29 million, or 91 percent, was invested in real estate mortgages, mostly farmlands.

The postwar agricultural depression of the 1920s had a dampening effect upon the company's commitment to farm loans as its almost total outlet for investment. The annual report of 1930 showed assets of nearly $149 million, but mortgage loans had shrunk from the high in 1917 of 91 percent down to 53 percent of the investment portfolio. Municipal and county bonds had grown dramatically to 22 percent of the total investment of the company's assets. Clearly the company was in the process of transition in its investment policies just at the moment that economic calamity struck the nation. The continuing Depression further stimulated this transition.

In 1932, with policyholders clamoring for loans in order to survive, the investment portfolio of the company read as follows: bonds, principally municipal and county bonds, 20 percent; first mortgage loans on real estate down to 45 percent; and policy loans up to 22 percent. As the country began its long struggle out of the Depression, the company once again, as it had in the very beginning, turned to United States Government bonds as a major area for its investment. "Company management," according to Patrick, "had become ultra conservative in investment matters." Property reluctantly acquired as a result of foreclosing mortgage loans, as detailed earlier in this history, was disposed of through an aggressive sales policy. For Fowler, the lessons learned in the 1930s would never be forgotten. By 1940, on the eve of America's wartime boom, the company's investment in farm mortgages had shrunk to 13 percent of its total investment portfolio.

The war-postwar decade of the 1940s, which Patrick has characterized as a period of "easy money, low interest rates and limited investment opportunities," saw an accentuation of the investment policies born out of the Depression. In 1946 the first postwar year, the company's investment in government securities and cash stood at 54 percent of the $386 million that the company had in assets; municipal bonds had dropped to 3 percent; and farm mortgages, from its once proud position of 90 percent of the portfolio, had now dropped to 7 percent. A long era, beginning in 1886, had ended. The company's investment policies in the second half of the twentieth century would, perhaps belatedly, reflect the changing appearance of the nation, a shift from an America of farms and small towns to an America of vast metropolitan regions, marked by the high-rise office buildings and condominiums of the central city and the sprawling fabricated housing, industrial parks, and shopping malls of suburbia.

Major social transitions are never easy, either for a nation in macrocosm or for the individual in microcosm. The deliberate decision of Bankers Life to reduce drastically its investment in farm loans in favor of loans that would take advantage of the opportunities that now lay in the city and its suburbs was as difficult for the company's investment field force to adjust to as had been for the sales agents to accept the earlier decisions of the company to change from being an assessment to a mutual company or to enter the group insurance field. As Patrick says in his history, "This decision was a great shock to the older, experienced men in the farm loan group, and many, many meetings and long hours were spent in explaining and justifying it to them. They felt downgraded—farm lending was based on studying a complex business and analyzing a food-producing plant. City residential lending was a simple business comparatively and thus far less interesting to the fieldmen. All one could say was it provided a significantly higher return." But that was all that needed to be said. This change, too, was as inevitable, if the company was to survive and prosper in the 1960s and 1970s, as was the decision to enter the group insurance field had been in 1941. By 1960, when the total assets of the company for the first time passed the $1 billion mark, city loans made up 41 percent of those invested assets and farm loans had dropped to just under 5 percent.

The rapid growth of group insurance further accelerated the company's assets and gave to the investment department an even more significant role in the operations of the company. Pension funds put extraordinary new demands upon the investment officials to find new outlets for these funds that would provide high yield without being high risk. Certainly, the rapidly expanding economy of the 1960s greatly facilitated their task, but the wide range of opportunities available made prudent and wise judgments even more imperative. In 1960, for the first time in its history, Bankers Life began to invest in common stock. Although stocks were not to be a substantial portion of its portfolio, the decision to invest in them at all represented a major break with the past.

By the end of the prosperous 1960s, the company's investment portfolio bore little resemblance to those that either Simon Casady or George Fowler had designed: United States Government bonds made up only 5 percent of the total investments, municipal and other local government bonds were 3 percent of the total; public utility, railroad, and industrial investments, 28 percent; city mortgage loans were up to 42 percent, the largest single area of investment; stocks (by this time, mostly common stock) 7 percent; while farm loans had virtually disappeared, making up only 1 percent of the total. A great deal of American history is encapsulated in these shifting percentage figures of one company's investments from 1887 to 1970. They capture in essence the changes that had occurred in America over a century of time, changes brought about by technological progress, by immigration, industrialization, and the cruel exigencies of depression and war.

During the long years that first Casady and then Fowler had directed the investment operations of the company, Bankers Life had established a deserved reputation throughout the insurance industry of being ultraconservative in its investment policies. "Never a dollar lost on investments" had long been the company's proud boast, and it was quite factually true until the post World War I farm depression of the 1920s. When Robert Patrick took over from Fowler, it may have appeared to the industry that Bankers Life planned no basic change in its investment policy from that which had for sixty years been so firmly entrenched as to seem to be immutable. A former Rhodes scholar, Patrick had been first employed by Bankers Life as an actuarial student. In 1932 he was transferred to the investment department. George Fowler and the Depression itself were his instructors in the investment field, and neither would be a likely candidate to serve as a model for reckless speculation. Patrick by temperament and his own personal life-style seemed to fit very nicely into the conservative world that his predecessors had fashioned. It soon became apparent, however, that Bankers Life in 1945 had found a new and very different kind of investment manager, a man who proved as appropriate for the postwar period of economic expansion as had Fowler for the economic contraction of the 1930s. Patrick's great strength for these years of growth was his adaptability to changing conditions and demands. He had the courage to seek out new investment possibilities and the intelligence to be able to distinguish between what could be a high-yield opportunity and what might be a high-risk venture. The problems he faced were the exact opposite of those of his immediate predecessor, but they were no less complex and difficult. An abundance of money can be as challenging to an investment officer as a scarcity of funds. Fortunately for him, the four presidents under whom he served as director of investment operations, Nollen, McConney, Warters, and Bucknell, were men of vision who could also adapt to new situations and who were willing to let Patrick chart his own itinerary through the maze of investment finance, not bound by the dictates of the outdated maps of the past decades. As a result, Patrick began to take an aggressive posture in investment that surprised and challenged the company's bolder competitors and shocked those others who still adhered to the same investment policies that Casady and Fowler had practiced. Patrick opened up doors that led Bankers Life into new fields of investment: the commercial mortgage business and direct residential loans, which most other insurance companies had abandoned. Patrick built a field force for residential mortgage loan investment as effective in its area of operations as the old farm loan force had been in the 1910s and 1920s.

Closely associated with Patrick was his right-hand assistant, Howard F. Dean. In many ways these two men complemented each other. Patrick's greatest interests lay in general investment and money market developments, in the coordination of investment policies with overall company programs, and in the development of the investment organization and staff to carry out these policies and programs. Dean, who was a well-trained investment specialist, was particularly adept in analyzing individual investment offerings, especially corporate securities. Over the years, great respect and confidence developed between these two men and between them and their two senior mortgage loan associates, Gene McAnelly and Harve Handford. Much of the success of the investment operation, as one member of the department has observed, resulted from this trust.

The possibilities for new fields of investment that Patrick explored or suggested in these years would continue to be successfully exploited by Dean, who succeeded him, and by Roy Ehrle, the present senior vice-president in charge of investments. Some of the former farm loan men, such as Rickert and McAnelly, with their valuable experience in the farm loan area, proved equally able in the new commercial, city residential mortgage field. By the late 1970s the major states providing a market for residential loans were Colorado,

Illinois, and the rapidly growing Sun Belt states of California, Texas, and Florida. Insured or guaranteed by either the Federal Housing Authority or the Veterans Administration, these loans had the great advantage of being high-yield investments with low risk.

Bankers Life was a powerful enough leader in the field to be able to defy the well-established mortgage brokers by taking over the servicing charges on these loans previously delegated to the mortgage brokers. In the various lawsuits that this policy produced, Bankers Life successfully defended its position in every case. It might be added parenthetically that all of these new investment areas produced legal problems which would keep the company's general counsel, Dwight Brooke, and his successor, Herman Bailey, and their law staffs from ever feeling underemployed.

The rapid growth and diversity of the company's investments forced a major change in the organizational structure of the investment department in the 1960s. The preliminary formulation of this new organizational plan began as early as 1962, when Warters, as chairman of the Board and chief executive officer, reported to the full Board on plans for separate accounts for pension funds, with the money to be invested in equities. The creation of separate accounts, however, could not be a final solution to the organizational needs of the investment operations. In the last months of his presidency, on February 12, 1968, Bucknell received from the Board preliminary authorization to form a subsidiary company "whose primary purpose will be to act as a marketing organization for the sale of variable annuity contracts, mutual funds and other products." In April, Bucknell was elected chairman of the Board and chief executive officer, and Harold G. Allen was chosen to succeed him to the presidency. Two months later, on June 24, 1968, the Board took the final formal step by authorizing the company to sponsor "unit investment trusts (mutual funds) and to establish a wholly-owned subsidiary company to provide management and investment advisory services to such unit investment trusts."

In implementing the Board's action, the company created two subsidiaries: Bankers Life Equity Services Corporation (BLESCO) to act as the broker-dealer marketing arm for the funds, and Bankers Life Equity Management Company (BLEMCO) to act as investment adviser to the funds. A few years later, a downstream holding company subsidiary, Bankers Life Investment Company, was established to own the stock of the various subsidiary companies, which came to include, in addition to BLESCO and BLEMCO, two real estate companies, Patrician Associates, Inc., and Petula Associates, Ltd., for the purchase and management of real estate property, which would eventually include the development of industrial parks in the Los Angeles area and in Atlanta, Georgia.

Presently, the chief investment officer of Bankers Life, Senior Vice-President R. W. Ehrle, serves as president of three of these subsidiary companies—BLEMCO, Patrician Associates, and Petula Associates—while Senior Vice-President J. H. Elken serves as president of BLESCO. In addition to serving as chairman of the Board of the parent Bankers Life Investment Company, President Houser also serves as chairman for two of its subsidiaries and Ehrle serves as chairman of the other two. Thus are the subsidiary investment companies tied securely to their original sponsor and owner, The Bankers Life Company. Simon Casady, with the $200,000 he had in assets to invest when he took over the management of the Association's funds in 1887, could he have been given a prescient glimpse into the future, would have found all of this more unbelievable than any science fiction novel from the pen of Jules Verne of men landing on the moon.

The rapid growth of Bankers Life in the 1950s and 1960s had as dramatic an impact upon every other area of the company's operations as it had upon investment management. Fortunately, technological advancement kept pace with growth and, indeed, stimulated further growth. Nowhere is this better illustrated than in the data-processing system of the company. The pattern of an administrative system for any insurance company is basically the same. As J. G. Helkenn, Bankers Life's senior vice-president for planning and data processing, has defined it in his history, *A Century of Systems Development*, written for the company archives, "A system ... [is] an organized group of procedures, records, forms, etc., that constitute an operating entity." For an insurance company, Helkenn continues, "administrative systems ... cover the period from issuance through termination of the policy contract: the actual issuance of the contract, production and maintenance of the basic policy record, billing and collection of premiums and termination through claim, expiry, surrender or lapse." Edward Temple would have had no difficulty in understanding that statement, for that was the same basic administrative system he established when he issued the first certificates of membership in his Association in 1879. But, Helkenn adds, "While this overall view of administration is simple in concept, there are many complexities brought about by the demands of increasing volume, a changing policy portfolio, requirement of regulatory agencies, management information needs, and the introduction of business machines." It is these complexities of increasing volume and the introduction of machines to meet the demands of volume that have revolutionized the data-processing system of Bankers Life over the past century and particularly within the last twenty-five years.

When Edward Temple opened his first office for The Bankers Life Association in 1879, he may have had a typewriter as his only piece of modern office equipment, for the typewriter was beginning to come into general use in the late 1870s. But the typewriter would have been used only for business correspondence. The records and business accounts would have been entered into ledgers by hand, and the assessment certificates would go out to their proud owners, written like a diploma in a beautiful Spencerian script, a practice that would be maintained by Bankers Life for its policies long after it became a mutual legal reserve company in 1911.

The basic record for assessment contracts was the call record, which provided all of the necessary information on the individual Association member. A major advance in expediting the sending of notices was made late in the nineteenth century when the embossed plate was introduced. The embossed metal plate system, known by its trade name, Addressograph, remained the basic communication system of the company with its Association members and company policyholders until the mid-twentieth century.

Mechanization of processes began to appear in other parts of the operational system in the first decade of the twentieth century. A simple calculating machine was purchased in 1904, and in 1907 the Board authorized the Association to purchase its first adding machine for the sum of fifty dollars—a major investment in office management. In 1911 the first time clocks for office employees were introduced. The machine age was here.

When Bankers Life became a mutual legal reserve company in the same year that time clocks were introduced, the collection card became the basic record on its policyholders as the old call record had been for the Association members. As more information was needed, additional card systems were introduced. At first all of these records had to be prepared individually, but in 1920 the first duplicating process was introduced so that an entire set of records could be made from a single master. In the early 1920s the first punched card equipment was introduced, initially in the actuarial department, but soon it was adopted throughout the entire system.

Each of these mechanical innovations of the early twentieth century, the first adding machine, "spirit" Ditto duplicator, and punched card record were major advancements in the data processing. As they became refined and further developed, they greatly expedited both the keeping of records and the transaction of the regular business operations of the company. But they represented no major quantum jump in data processing. That leap would come in the mid-twentieth century with the introduction of the electronic computer.

Our moment of time in human history will undoubtedly have to be known as the age of the computer, for it has been the computer that has brought the kind of revolution to our society that is more total in its impact than was the introduction of steam power to the late eighteenth/early nineteenth century or the introduction of electricity and the invention of the internal-combustion engine to the late nineteenth/early twentieth century. It has been the computer that has enabled us to send missiles and men into space, that has made possible the collection, storage, and retrieval of data to affect and change every area of human inquiry. Certainly it has transformed business activity, making the impossible possible in terms of products, services, and planning. It is both servant and master of our age.

The age of the computer arrived for Bankers Life in May 1955 when the Executive Committee of the Board authorized the company to lease an IBM 650. The machine was installed in June 1956, and the formidable task of converting to the new system was begun. A separate "conversion division," employing some forty-seven people, was created, and after six years all of the information from the manual records for individual life policies had been converted into punched cards that could be fed into the machine. No sooner had this system been established, however, than advances in electronics made it obsolete. In 1962 the lease of IBM 7010 system was authorized and the "daily cycle" system was introduced. The punched card information was converted to magnetic tape, a new diet required by the new machine. The men responsible for inaugurating the age of the computer into Bankers Life operations, in addition to John Helkenn, were Leo Danzinger, John Sackett, and Bob Delaney. They were the new technicians for a completely new age.

The initial period of the electronic data processing was exclusively devoted to the transformation of the individual life system. Seeing the revolutionary change in processing that was occurring in that area, Archibald, Schneider, and Trowbridge were eager to introduce the same miracles of processing into the group insurance field. This seemed impossible, given the capabilities of the existing computers in the early 1970s. But clearly, the electronics field has a momentum all its own. Direct-access storage devices—data cells and magnetic disks—were being introduced which made technically possible the development and implementation of the Consolidated Group System (CGS). It was as if the aviation industry had leaped from the crude biplane the Wright Brothers had tested at Kitty Hawk in 1903 to the 747 jet plane in only ten years.

"This improved equipment plus the experience gained from earlier efforts in the individual insurance area," according to Helkenn, "made the approach to CGS a deliberate business policy decision. The concept at the outset was to develop a 'consolidated' system to provide for the administration of Group Life, Health and Pension products. A number of Group Department personnel were transferred to planning, among them Don Carter, now Vice President of the Group Life and Health Department, who headed the project." On December 8, 1975, the Executive Committee of the Board authorized the company to purchase additional IBM equipment at a cost in excess of $5 million—more than the total cost of the home office building in 1940, it might be added. With Helkenn's and his associates' technological knowledge and with Carter's awareness of the processing needs for the entire group insurance field, the CGS system that resulted remains to this day unique in the industry and has given Bankers Life a decided advantage in the group insurance field. "By the late 1970s," Helkenn writes, in concluding his short history of a major technological revolution, "CGS had reached a state of 'flexible, changing, maturity.' Conversion of all products was complete and all major functions were mechanized. However, with the near astronomical growth of business (particularly in the pension area) in a changing world, much work was still being done to adjust to new situations and it appeared that much more would continue—indefinitely." The giant memory bank on the fourth floor of the home office building purrs on, quietly ingesting new data, forgetting nothing that it has taken in and ready at a second's notice to tell all. Bankers Life today is light-years away from Mr. Stilson and his two-inch pencils.

Helkenn in his history of Bankers Life systems developments makes the important observation that a major significance of the introduction of the computer "from the systems planning point of view is that it inaugurated the 'Consolidated Functions' approach to administrative activity.... During the first 75 to 80 years of The Bankers Life's existence, there was a gradual movement in the opposite direction as our business grew in volume and complexity." For example, in the beginning there had been one collection card that contained all of the basic information for each contract, and this single card was used for all of the process operations involved with that contract. But "as the business grew in volume and complexity, additional records were created for each separate function: an Addressograph plate file, a separate policy loan file, a reserve valuation file, a mortality research file, an abstract for first year accounting, etc. With separate files of information came the exposure to inconsistency of information and the need to cross verify these data continually, an additional expenditure of time and effort and naturally increased cost. The computer, with its internal processing capability, provided the means to bring these activities back together, reducing duplication and engendering the term 'Consolidated Functions Approach.'"

Yet viewed from another perspective, the computer can be regarded as a centrifugal, not a centripetal, force. There are now computer terminals in over one hundred agency offices across the nation with a tie-in to the computer facilities in the home office. With this direct access to the data bank, these agency offices can obtain printed sales illustrations, make policy loans, and provide policyholders with current data on their policies. It is anticipated that eventually these agency offices with computer terminal facilities will be able to settle claims and pay benefits due. "Further illustration of this 'outreach' view," as Helkenn points out, "is embodied in the continued enhancement of the Consolidated Group System. There are now fifteen regional claim offices across the country, with five to fifty computer terminals each, connected to the computer in the Home Office by communication lines and engaged in the processing and payment of group health claims."

The computer has played a significant role for the company quite apart from its function in data processing. As Helkenn implies in his history, the computer has become the essential tool for the actuaries and planning officers in making long-range projections and in the development of new products, for it can provide a new dimension of knowledge to that central concern of all insurance companies—how to play successfully that old game posed by Pascal, the game of probabilities.

As has been emphasized repeatedly throughout this history, Bankers Life has been an actuarially oriented company ever since the

Nollen brothers brought their mathematical skills to the service of the company at the turn of the century. Every president, from Nollen on, began his employment in the company within the actuarial department. And Bankers Life has had an influence upon actuarial science and its professional organizations far beyond that which the actual size of the company's actuarial department would warrant. Three Bankers Life officers have served as presidents of the Society of Actuaries: Edmund McConney as its first president in 1949, after having successfully achieved the union of the two previously rival organizations, the Actuarial Society of America and the American Institute of Actuaries; Dennis Warters, who became president of the society in 1960; and the present senior vice-president and chief actuary, C. L. Trowbridge, who served as president of the society in 1975. Thus has the profession and the insurance industry recognized Bankers Life's preeminent role in the basic science of insurance.

The impact of the computer upon the capabilities of this science has been nothing short of "fantastic," according to Trowbridge. Suddenly, a whole new world had been opened up to the actuary. As Trowbridge says, "The actuary's job today is far less mathematical, far more mechanical, and infinitely more sophisticated. We can do things now because we have the data that could never have been done in the past. It is a major research tool."

But the computer, for all of its potential, is simply a tool. It is only as good as the men and women who program it for use. Bankers Life was innovative in its products long before it had a computer because it had planners and developers with innovative ideas and managerial leadership who did not fear new ideas. To illustrate this, one can point to three new products in the individual life field that Bankers Life has offered in the past twenty years. All three were to have a major impact upon the industry; all three were the result of imaginatively new and even daring approaches to old concerns within the individual life insurance field.

The first of these new products, which came to be known as the Guaranteed Purchase Option (GPO), was developed before the computer had become a research tool. Field agents had long pressed for something their customers had frequently asked for—a means by which an individual policyholder might increase his or her insurance as financial responsibilities grew without running the risk of being refused on medical grounds. These repeated suggestions of the field force found a proponent in Bob Shay, who in the early 1950s served as director of agencies. Shay was able to interest the actuarial department in this possibility, and by 1957 Bankers Life was prepared to go into the market with a new option for ordinary life policies by which, for a small extra premium, a policyholder would be able to purchase additional insurance at specific periods of time and for specific amounts without a new medical examination or without any questions being asked as to the policyholder's current state of health.

On December 6, 1957, Bankers Life carried a bold, full-page ad in *Eastern Underwriter*, followed by the same ad in *National Underwriter* the next day. "First to Offer This *Brand New Concept*," the advertisement carried as its headline. "Now one physical examination carries you through the years! A revolutionary new idea that guarantees your 'insurability' to age 40 ... gives you the *right* to buy added insurance at standard rates, regardless of health ... And only Bankers Life of Des Moines has it!" But not for long. It was an idea whose time had long since come. It became a best seller for Bankers Life, and very quickly almost every other life insurance company, under one name or another, was offering the Guaranteed Purchase Option to its customers.

The GPO had been developed with little help from the computer as a research tool. The task of the actuarial planners was certainly made immeasureably easier and the results were far more sophisticated, however, in the development of Bankers Life's two other major innovations in individual life in the past two decades. At about the same time that the GPO benefit was ready for the market, Warters, almost as if he were anticipating the computer age with all of its challenging opportunities, assigned Bill Rae and a bright young actuary named John Taylor to devote their entire time to development. Warters wanted from them new products for the immediate future, new ideas and new directions for the company for the long-range future. Rae had already proven himself to Warters with his early work in the group insurance field, particularly in implementing Warters' ideas for group permanent insurance. Some officers of the company today regard Rae as having been the most brilliant actuary to have ever served that department in its long history of achievement for the company. And in Taylor, Rae had precisely the right associate.

Within a short time, Rae and Taylor were able to come up with a revolutionary new product, a simple participating ordinary life policy but with its premiums approximately the same as the rates for nonparticipating policies sold by the stock insurance companies such as Aetna or Travelers. Stock companies had always had something of an advantage over the mutual life companies inasmuch as they could offer a kind of insurance that is known in the trade as a nonparticipating (or nonpar) policy. Such a policy provided life protection but paid no dividends. Because of this, the nonpar policy could be offered at a lower rate of premium than that for participating policies. Mutual companies, however, have traditionally paid dividends on their ordinary life policies. Their policyholders were participants, through dividends, in the surplus distribution of their companies. Participating policies of necessity, then, had to have higher gross premiums than nonparticipating policies—or so top management everywhere thought.

Field agents, to be sure, had long chafed under the competition that nonpar policies presented, and as early as 1957 the Agency Managers' Advisory Committee had urged the company to develop an ordinary life policy with a low gross premium which would be competitive with nonpar policies. Rae and Taylor now set to work on the problem. Given the company's phenomenal growth, and particularly its growth in assets, and given the success of the investment force in producing a high rate of return on those investments, why couldn't the company cut its premium costs to the policyholder down to approximately the same level as non-par policies, and still offer dividends? The policyholder could thus eat his cake, frosted with dividends, and have it, too. On July 30, 1962, the Board was informed that the company was now ready to offer a new "low-premium," special whole life policy at essentially nonparticipating rates. This announcement startled the entire insurance industry as nothing had since Bankers Life announced a group permanent policy in the early 1940s. The new "low-rate" policy was, quite naturally, an immediate success. It revitalized the individual ordinary life insurance business for the company. And with a product as attractive as this was to the market, Bankers Life not only won the plaudits of its own agency force but also for the first time successfully caught the attention of the important insurance brokers for its individual life policies. Earl Bucknell, who was president at the time this major breakthrough was made, quite correctly saw in the development of this one new product a graphic illustration of how the close interrelationship of many areas within the company can successfully produce a major breakthrough in insurance products. "How was it possible for Bankers Life Company to sell a policy with those premiums and then pay annual dividends too?" he would later write. "Only if the Investment Department could continue to produce an increasingly favorable return on investments, and if operational expenses could be adequately controlled (by effective use of such things as the computer, the work management program to control costs) and only if the sales department could sell it in increasing quantity. So its success depended upon top grade management in at least three areas—and actually some others such as underwriting and sales promotion." Imagination, planning, management, investment, promotion, and sales—it was a neat, total package, tied up with the blue ribbon of success.

Later this low gross premium principle was extended to a few other individual life plans—Life at 65 Moneysaver (1966) and Century 100 (1973). Although this principle was not widely copied by other companies, as was the GPO concept, "it may well have been," according to Trowbridge, "the genesis of the Economatic policy which was introduced by others a few years later."

The third major innovation in individual life was definitely a product of the computer age. It, too, was born of the field agents' demand for a more flexible individual life insurance policy, one that could go much further in meeting changing individual needs than the GPO did, valuable as that option had proved to be. Lambert Trowbridge, who had returned to the actuarial department to reassume President Houser's previous responsibilities for individual policy development, was intrigued by this idea of a truly flexible policy. Would it be possible to harness the computer equipment to the task of providing data that would substantiate the feasibility of producing an individual policy so flexible that the changing needs of the policyholder could be met? The usual name given to this concept was the "life cycle" idea. What was meant by that poetic but vague term was a policy that could change in face amount or in level of premium and hence could expand or contract as the insurance needs of the policyowner, and the ability to pay, varied throughout a person's life. It was as intriguing but seemingly as impossible of achievement as the dream of a perpetual-motion machine. Trowbridge was ready, however, to attempt to square this particular circle. With the preliminary details worked out by early 1974, he went with his plan to the Product Evaluation Committee, at that moment chaired by Senior Vice-President Merv Cramer. According to Trowbridge, Cramer gave the green light. "Cramer felt in his bones that the idea was in the consumer's interest. With Cramer's support, the basic concept was accepted by the Product Evaluation Committee."

A few months later, Trowbridge was far enough along with the new concept that the Product Evaluation Committee, by then under the chairmanship of John Elken, was able to present to top management a task force's recommendation that Bankers Life establish a leadership position in an industry-wide effort to develop a life cycle policy. At that time it was felt that Bankers Life by itself did not have the resources to solve all of the many problems connected with the development and marketing of such a policy, particularly in securing the various state insurance commissions' approval. Then in December 1974, according to Trowbridge, "We got a real surprise. We discovered that Minnesota Mutual (without any fanfare and with almost no industry recognition) already had such a product on the market—and that it had issued what it called Adjustable Life (on a piece-meal basis) since 1971." The sentiments at that moment within Bankers Life must have been similar to those felt by Charles Darwin upon reading Alfred Wallace's little article outlining the entire theory of evolution just prior to Darwin's going to press with *The Origin of Species.*

Plans to present Trowbridge's concepts to the insurance industry for its general development were quickly scrapped. "Since Minnesota Mutual had already solved several of the most difficult problems," Trowbridge recalls, "Bankers Life should now go gung-ho on its own development. This would not really be a copy of Minnesota Mutual, since we had developed much of the theory independently, and had some improvements of our own....The organizational structure for what would be a massive developmental effort was a series of five task forces, reporting to Trowbridge and Elken. Through the combined effort of actuarial, EDP, policyholder services, market research, agency department and marketing services personnel, Bankers Life's adjustable life policy went on the market on January 1, 1977."

By providing for the kind of flexibility the field agents had long asked for on behalf of their customers, in which individual policyholders could periodically change both premium costs and coverage from term to whole life, The Bankers Life adjustable life was given nationwide attention, not only in the insurance journals but also in such general publications as *The Wall Street Journal, Forbes, Changing Times, and Consumer Reports.* The public relations department did yeoman service in publicizing the policy, and the response was more gratifying than even the men who had developed it—Trowbridge, Cramer, Elken, Freeman, and Gene Reifsnider—might have anticipated. Within two years of its appearance on the market, the adjustable life plan had captured nearly 40 percent of Bankers

Life's new individual life insurance sales.

New products born of management's ingenuity and the computers' efficiency were not the exclusive monopoly of the individual life field, however. Illustrative of this was the company's decision to enter the property liability insurance field. Early in 1970 Taylor began his systematic study of this possibility. For this study, he drew upon the experience of those companies already in the field and upon the published reports of insurance experts such as Bernard Webb, associate professor of Actuarial Science and Insurance at Georgia State University. He was greatly aided by the research of his own staff, in particular by that of Dorothy Payne, who as assistant secretary of corporate planning would soon have the honor of becoming one of the first women officers in the history of the company. In December 1970 Taylor made his initial report on the subject, a report that had been prepared with the same exacting attention to detail as that which Warters had given to the Board in 1940 in considering the question as to whether or not Bankers Life should enter the group insurance field. The pros and cons for property liability insurance were listed and carefully evaluated. The arguments against entering the field seemed the more weighty, however. They included such reasons as the following:

"It is better to concentrate on what we do well. We would spread ourselves too thin were we to enter the property insurance field.... A substantial amount of money would be required initially to enter the property insurance field. The alternative uses for our policyowners' funds would be more beneficial to them." In May 1971 Taylor wrote a formal memo to President Allen, concluding in summary, "We recommend that we do not enter the property-liability insurance field now. We think that conditions are likely to develop at some time within the next five or ten years that will make desirable our starting a property insurance company to sell automobile insurance and homeowners insurance on a group basis." He assured Allen that he and his staff would "continue to review the property-liability insurance field, keeping in touch with current developments."

Taylor did continue his review, and conditions continued to develop much more rapidly than he had anticipated. The market grew rapidly, and as many states began to introduce "no-fault" auto insurance laws, the legal picture greatly changed. By 1973 Taylor had accumulated a new set of data and had arrived at a quite different conclusion. In his report to the company, dated April 10, 1973, he concluded: "Entering the property-liability insurance field—and more specifically the fields of mass and group automobile and homeowners insurance and personal umbrella liability—is not without risks. There are also substantial potential rewards, financially and in the form of additional insurance services to present and potential policyholders. We would conclude that the field is proper for entry by Bankers Life Company under the terms and philosophy we have outlined." On June 25, 1973, the Board approved of the entry of Bankers Life into the property liability field. A subsidiary company, as required by Iowa law, had to be created for the marketing of "automobile casualty and liability policies and homeowners and multiple peril policies," with marketing assistance expected to come from Bankers Life's group department and from agents and brokers. In February 1974 the new subsidiary company, the BLC Insurance Company, with an initial capitalization of $3 million, began operations as a part of the cluster of subsidiary companies under the aegis of The Bankers Life Investment Company. The personnel for this new company was drawn almost entirely from within Bankers Life's own staff. Donald Krieg was made president of the new company and William Schneider became chairman of the company's Board of Directors. In November 1974 Bankers Life offered its first mass-marketed automobile insurance policy to its own employees, and a homeowners policy the following April. Its marketing policies were unique within the field. Property liability was not sold directly to the individual but rather only through sponsoring organizations, such as associations, credit unions, or by employers, as part of an increasingly standard form of employee benefits. Under Krieg's forceful management, the growth in sales of property liability has justified Bankers Life's decision to enter the field. The subsidiary company has even more ambitious goals for the future. By the end of Bankers Life's centennial year in 1979, the property liability company hopes to have quadrupled the number of policies it had in force in 1976.

Once again the company had dramatically illustrated its ability to adapt successfully to the ever-changing field of insurance, not by plunging recklessly into any new proposal that held out glittering promises of material gain, but rather through careful research and planning, arriving at a rational decision which could then deliver on its data-supported promises.

Under the direction of John Taylor and with the active encouragement of Presidents Allen and Houser, Bankers Life has continued to study the question of diversification, of new areas it might enter, of other areas it should avoid. In February 1973 Taylor made a report on

"Results of Diversification Survey," based on replies he had received from some thirty life insurance companies throughout the nation. Included in the possible areas of diversification were the following fields: variable life insurance (individual and group); variable annuities; mutual funds; closed-end bond funds; real estate investment trusts; workmen's compensation and commercial multi-peril insurance; various professional services such as investment management, actuarial, pension, and medical plan administration, and computer services; reinsurance; banking; finance companies; and health maintenance organizations. Under each category of possible diversification were listed those companies, if any, having that particular area already in operation, those companies developing plans in that area, those giving study to the area, and those who were not interested. Here were potentials for possible expansion and growth which might well engage Bankers Life for a major portion of its second century of existence, and out of which undoubtedly would emerge many new products and services it would in the future offer to its customers. Neither the planners nor the computer need ever be idle.

The phenomenal growth of Bankers Life in the past two decades has had an obvious impact upon personnel throughout the organization both in numbers of people employed and in the skills and training demanded of them. First to be considered among the personnel are the three men who presided over the company during these years and gave to its growth the direction and stimulation it needed. The immediate successor to Warters as president was Earl Bucknell, who was elected president in 1961. Bucknell's assumption of the presidency had a beneficial impact upon the morale of both the home office staff and the sales field and within the community at large. Fully appreciative of Warters' great strengths and contributions to the company, Bucknell at the same time was clearly sensitive to the necessary changes that had to come from the top down. Interoffice communications had to be opened up. Responsible subordinates had to be encouraged to take stands and then to be supported in their decisions. Whatever corrective steps in respect to a single individual's actions that might need to be taken should be done as privately and discreetly as possible; whatever praise that might be merited by any individual should be given as freely and in as public a forum as possible. This was Bucknell's program for a new order, and he was remarkably successful in implementing it. In many ways, Bucknell represents as dramatic a transition in the history of the company's presidency as did Kuhns and Nollen in respect to their predecessors. Highly civic-minded, Bucknell did much to reestablish the company's reputation for service within the community that Nollen had so successfully maintained for two decades. Philanthropic contributions to education and service organizations within the city and state were greatly increased and the method of distributing grants was systematically formalized by the establishment of a committee on corporate contributions.

Bucknell also went out into the field, and got to know and be known by the agents. Once again the agents felt they had a man in the president's chair who knew their problems firsthand. Tensions, here, too, began to dissipate.

Bucknell was able to create a tone and style within the company that not only have persisted but have been strengthened by his two successors. Harold Allen, who became president in 1968, and Robert Houser, who succeeded Allen in 1973, were to continue the basic managerial policies established by Bucknell. Both were to stress open communications within the home office and between the home office and the field. Both were not only receptive to, but aggressively pushed, innovation through planning and development. To build upon the pioneer work done in long-range planning by Patrick under Bucknell's presidency, upon Patrick's retirement in 1971, Allen asked John Taylor to take charge of long-range planning. The philosophy that Taylor was to develop for corporate planning fit very well into the basic philosophy of the company as envisioned by Bucknell, Allen, and Houser: "Of keeping management informed," as Taylor has expressed it, "about the business environment in which they operate and the interface of business to society in such a way that management can make better decisions today about the activities which are going to affect the company tomorrow."

The three presidencies of Bucknell, Allen, and Houser, covering nearly two decades of the company's history, represent a remarkable continuum in style and policy, even though the three have differed considerably in individual personality. All three have made a point of keeping in close touch with the field force. The agents have greatly appreciated their efforts and their genuine concern for their welfare.

Under Allen and Houser, the company has achieved the most spectacular growth in its history and, indeed, has set records for rate of growth within the industry (see Appendix). One of Bucknell's proudest boasts is that the company has doubled in size in the ten years since he left office. This could not have been accomplished without Allen's and Houser's planning for it, encouraging it by innovations and, above all, finding the right personnel to implement it. Houser, in a recent memorandum, has best summed up the achievements of the company when he wrote to a colleague: "The original goals of Edward Temple seem now to be reaching fruition. Among these I would list the following: (1) Low cost; (2) Innovative products; (3) Aggressive merchandising; (4) True mutuality with customers' interests first; (5) Complete integrity."

Not a bad checklist for any company to have before it, and much of the credit for being able to put a check mark in the right column for each item on this list must be given to Bucknell, Allen, and Houser. But certainly not the total credit. Successful management cannot depend upon a single individual. All three of these presidents were to be greatly dependent upon those individuals whom they had inherited from the Nollen, McConney, and Warters regimes as well as upon those whose talents they themselves had discovered and encouraged: Executive Vice-President John Taylor; Senior Investment Officer Roy Ehrle; General Counsels Dwight Brooke and Herman Bailey; Chief Actuary Lambert Trowbridge; Senior Vice-President Bill Schneider along with Bob Larson, Dave Hurd, Don Krieg, and Don Carter in the group life, health, and pension field; or Senior Vice-President John Elken and Bob Freeman, Gene Reifsnider, and Jack Watson in individual life. Nor can successful management depend only upon top management, however valuable their services and contributions may be. It is dependent upon the salesmen in the field and upon the employees within the home office, skilled and unskilled, who make up the entire Bankers Life organization. Personnel considerations must always be a major concern for any company, and Bankers Life's personnel story is certainly an essential part of its history.

When Bankers Life moved into its new home office building in the spring of 1940, it had 515 home office employees, a number that had remained fairly constant since the mid-1920s. During the next five years that number would actually shrink, reaching a low of 383 in 1943 as male employees were drafted for military service and as the competition for female employees became much more intense in the general labor market.

Bankers Life, since at least the turn of the century, had always been greatly dependent upon women for its home office personnel, for beginning with the introduction of the typewriter in the late nineteenth century, women had increasingly dominated the office clerical field, almost as completely as they had come to dominate elementary school teaching following the Civil War. Up until World War II, Bankers Life had had little difficulty in recruiting female office personnel. Hundreds of young women, fresh out of high school and eager to leave their small Iowa hometowns, had flocked to the big city to seek jobs and, as many hoped, eventually husbands. Des Moines was a city of insurance companies, and insurance companies needed a great many clerical workers. At Bankers Life, Equitable of Iowa and the many other home and branch insurance offices in the city, these women found employment. In terms of numbers alone, they dominated the insurance office personnel field. Nearly 80 percent of the home office personnel at Bankers Life by the late 1920s were women.

Sheer numbers, however, do not represent corresponding power in the business field. Women might constitute the overwhelming majority of employees within the insurance industry, but as with all other businesses, insurance was a male-dominated world. Bankers Life might be a generous employer in terms of providing clerical job opportunities at a relatively favorable wage and hour scale, but as with almost all other companies, the doors leading to the higher levels of management were firmly locked to women. In those distant pre-women's liberation days, no one thought it strange that in personnel memoranda, the hundreds of women employees within the home office were almost always referred to as "girls." Girls they were when they entered the company's employment right out of high school and girls they remained no matter how long they stayed with the company.

Unfortunately, they did not stay very long if they asserted their maturity by marrying. From the time the first woman was hired, Bankers Life had had a standing personnel policy that immediately upon marriage, the woman's employment with the company was terminated, and during the Depression years this was considered to be a highly responsible social policy. In 1941, due to the wartime labor shortage, however, this policy was modified to allow married women to stay on as temporary employees. They were designated as Temporary-D employees, with the "D" standing for duration. Even after the war, however, when the company continued to employ married women on a temporary basis, Bankers Life's strict rule still prevailed. It would not be until 1962 that Warters abruptly terminated all restrictions upon the employment of married women, even those who subsequent to their employment had married fellow home office employees.

Discriminatory regulations against married women now read like documents from an ancient history. Not only does the company presently allow married women to retain their jobs, but beginning in 1966 it innovated a new recruitment policy that actively sought out married women. In August of that year, the company inserted a small advertisement in the *Des Moines Sunday Register* addressed to "Mothers of School Children." It read in part:

> *How'd you like to be able to help with family expenses by working in our home office from approximately 9 A.M. to 3 P.M.? You can start as early as September 6 and work until school's out next June (or longer if you prefer) and then return the following September if you like.... You'll be able to get your husband off to work and your children off to school and get home in the afternoon in time to care for them when they return.... We'll help you get your skills back up to top-notch capacity with good training on the job.*

The response to this single advertisement far exceeded the hopes of its sponsors, Ray Cassell and Dalles Schroeder. Bankers Life had imaginatively struck a gold mine of a largely untapped labor reserve. The so-called "9 til' 3" plan has provided the company with continuing supply of mature, often highly trained women who had given up their previous employment in order to become mothers. Many of these women have returned each September as soon as the school doors were opened, and some became full-time permanent employees as their children grew older.

It was not only the "9 til' 3" employees who were to benefit from a more flexible workday, however. In April 1974 Chief Executive Officer Allen introduced the "flexible hours" concept on a trial basis. Under this plan, an employee with the supervisor's approval might elect his or her own hours from a wide range beginning with one workday that started at 7:00 A.M. and finished at 3:45 P.M. up to one for the late arisers that began at 9:00 A.M. and finished at 5:45 P.M. So successful was this trial innovation that it has been continued ever since, for the law of averages seems to operate here as effectively as it does in every other field where human choice is given a wide range.

These innovative personnel policies that Bankers Life has introduced in the last two decades are indicative of the growing pressure that all large companies have faced in the expansive postwar years in recruiting able personnel. Of far greater value to the company in its recruitment efforts and in retaining personnel was its policy of providing liberal fringe benefits. As early as 1940 it provided a pension plan for its home office personnel. Two years later, group hospital and surgical benefits were added and soon thereafter, group life and group dental. Both pension and health benefits have been steadily increased to keep pace with the rising cost of living. The medical plan subsequently provided for pregnancy benefits, thus putting Bankers Life in advance of some other large companies and recent Supreme Court rulings, and beginning in 1973 employees were given a fifteen-day salary continuance "during disability related to maternity and childbirth." The company had come a long way from the time when marriage meant instant dismissal for the woman employee.

In spite of these liberal policies, however, the rapid expansion of the company and the growing complexities of its business kept the personnel officers under constant pressure to recruit and train new employees. The personnel department was reorganized in the 1960s and under the able direction of R. E. Cassell, secretary of the company and senior vice-president, was merged with general services as a division of corporate services. Prior to World War II, recruitment had never been a major problem for the home office, but by the spring of 1960 personnel began for the first time the active recruitment of high school students. Visits by the personnel staff were made to many of the high schools in Des Moines and the surrounding communities, and regularly scheduled tours of the home office building for high school seniors were instituted.

Once the new recruit was hired, personnel also had to be concerned with the far more complicated task of on-the-job training and of evaluating the employee's performance on the job. Although the company had conducted many short training programs in the past, it was not until 1972 that Dal Schroeder developed a centralized training area with programs in orientation, leadership, and supervisor development. The company also encouraged its home office personnel to further their formal higher education by providing two thirds of the cost of tuition at an accredited college or professional school. In 1965 the personnel department also began the "Supervisors' Work Management Program." A national firm, the Booz-Allen Methods Services, Inc., was brought in to train a group of Bankers Life employees who in turn could "train supervisors and their assistants in the techniques of work analysis and to assist them in applying these techniques within their departments." In 1972 the work management unit was made a division of corporate services. Also, in 1973 the job evaluation program was greatly strengthened by the expansion of the Hay System to apply not only to officers but to all employees throughout the company.

The growing social awareness of the nation in the 1960s and the resulting federal legislation in respect to discrimination were also to have a major impact upon the personnel policies of Bankers Life. In 1968 a group of Des Moines business leaders formed the Greater Des Moines Merit Employers Council. Chief Executive Officer Bucknell in announcing Bankers Life's active participation in this council told the officers and supervisors of the company that "the purpose of the Council is to encourage merit employment in the Des Moines area, without regard to race, color, religion, sex or national origin, and to provide equal opportunity for all employees. Our own Company is taking an active part in the Council's activities...." The council held a series of job opportunity seminars for high school seniors and their parents to encourage them to seek employment among the participating businesses in the council. Bankers Life also became an active supporter of YES (Youth Employment Service), as a part of the New Horizons Program. Beginning in the summer of 1973, the company employed young people from disadvantaged backgrounds to work in various departments throughout the home office.

Bankers Life's participation in these various programs for the disadvantaged was an admirable gesture of goodwill, but it was a minor palliative at best. A far more systematic approach to the problem was needed. In February 1973, in response to an Iowa Civil Rights Commission complaint, President Allen announced a new program of affirmative action in nondiscriminatory employment practices. "Our affirmative action program," he told the home office staff, "is designed to assure equal opportunity to all persons in the areas of recruiting and hiring, working conditions, training programs, promotions, upgrading, advancement, use of Company facilities, and in all other terms, conditions and privileges of employment."

In August 1976 this affirmative action program was greatly strengthened by President Houser's appointment of an equal employment opportunity supervisor, who has since worked with each department in the home office and with each sales region to use a coordinator for the supervision of hiring practices and to set goals and establish timetables for the achievement of those goals. In 1973, when the affirmative action program was established, the minority hiring rate for home office personnel was less than 4 percent. By 1977 it had reached 10 percent. Bankers Life still had a long way to go to reach its overall corporate objective of having 5 percent of its personnel belonging to minority racial groups, but a promising start had at last been made.

Slowly, too, new opportunities were made available to women within the home office staff and considerable progress has been made in the decade of the 1970s. In 1973 only 11 percent of the women employees had a company title. By 1977 that figure had risen to over 30 percent and four women had become officers of the company. In part, this change in status of women within the company is because women are entering the company's employment with much higher educational qualifications. Prior to 1973, less than 10 percent of the women hired by the company each year were college graduates. By 1977, 50 percent of all the college graduates hired by the company were women. There were now women available in nearly every department of the company who had the educational background and skills to compete effectively with their male counterparts for managerial positions. The "girls" of the 1930s and 1940s had come a long way.

Programs designed to promote the hiring of qualified women and minorities were not entirely altruistically motivated. As the company continued its remarkable expansion in the postwar years it needed an ever-increasing number of able people in every department within the home office from whatever labor pools there might be available. In 1950 there were 600 employees in the home office. Ten years later that number had increased by 66 percent. The addition to the home office building, which had been completed in 1959, was already filled to capacity. In 1964 the Board authorized the construction of a large annex across Seventh Street, which would be connected with the home office building by a sky walk. That, too, was quickly filled, and by June 1975, with 1,881 home office employees seeking space and a projected figure of 2,400 employees by 1980, plans were begun for the construction of a major addition which would complete the quadrangle on High and Eighth streets as originally envisioned in the late 1930s. It was hoped that the opening of this addition, which would add 150,000 square feet of floor space, could be effected by the time that the company celebrated its centennial in June 1979. There was no question but that it would be quickly and fully utilized.

These years of growth also saw dramatic changes in both

quantity and quality for the field personnel as well as in the home office staff. As detailed earlier, the individual and group insurance fields each developed their own sales organizations, although Bankers Life agents were utilized by the group sales organization to sell group insurance and pensions as well as individual life insurance. The rapid development of group insurance, with its reliance for much of its sales production on brokers, accelerated the entry of the brokerage agency into individual policy sales. Attracted first by Bankers Life group permanent policies, and later by its low-premium special whole life policies, insurance brokers became increasingly interested in handling Bankers Life products. By 1978 approximately one third of Bankers Life individual insurance was sold through brokerage agencies of the individual sales organization. There were in all thirty-one individual brokerage agencies throughout the country selling Bankers Life insurance.

The career agencies have remained central, however, to Bankers Life's individual policy sales force, selling two thirds of its insurance. These ninety-four central career agencies are divided into five regions, covering all fifty states in the nation. Both the agency managers and the individual agents have in recent years had good reason to believe that in Merwyn Cramer and his successor, John Elken, they have had a powerful voice of support in the home office. Close relations have also been maintained with the home office through Bob Freeman, the present agency vice-president, whom Cramer had brought in from Metropolitan as regional director of agencies. With his background, Freeman was able to bring to his job a knowledge of both marketing and financial operations. Jack Watson, vice-president in charge of individual insurance operations, although not directly concerned with the sales force, is also essential to its effectiveness. Watson, with a background in advertising and public relations, had at one time served as president of the industry's Life Advertisers Association. He was also an old friend of most of the career agents, partly because he was at one time sales promotion director in charge of arranging for all sales conventions, succeeding John Grimes in that position. These experiences and his own concern for service to the policyholders proved invaluable assets in his job.

The present-day newly recruited field agent is of a somewhat different breed than his predecessors of the 1920s and 1930s—generally more sophisticated, with more formal education, and having a higher quality of specific training for his or her job. In 1960 Ray Hamill, who had succeeded Ted Tomlinson as director of training, reorganized the entire sales training program at Bankers Life with Cramer's active encouragement. The whole thrust of training was broadened to include not only agents but agency managers. The concept of the canned, hard-sell speech was deemphasized, and stress was now put upon the agent serving the individual customer as a financial consultant as well as a seller of insurance policies. Hamill brought in Gene Reifsnider as his assistant, and upon Hamill's retirement due to poor health, Reifsnider succeeded him, eventually becoming vice-president of marketing services. In this position, Reifsnider along with his staff has provided the individual field force with marketing services that have helped to keep the company in the forefront of the rapidly changing and highly competitive market for individual insurance. If there are today few agency managers who are quite as colorful as the Frasers, Martins, Bowmans, and the "Pop" Reeds of the past, they are far better trained in the presentation of Bankers Life products to their communities, and many of them, such as Dick Olson, the present mayor of Des Moines, play significant roles of leadership in their communities.

There has, however, been a continuity with the past. Two generations of Bankers Life agents have not been an uncommon phenomenon: the Martins of Ottumwa, Iowa, and the Frasers of Lincoln, Nebraska. Illustrative of this tradition, which has continued into the present, are the Hendricksons of the small south-central Nebraska town of Holdrege. Carl Hendrickson first joined Bankers Life as an agent in 1925 and quickly became one of their top salesmen. His son, Bruce, after graduating from the University of Nebraska and serving a stint in the Navy, came back to join his father in the office at Holdrege. From the first year of selling, Bruce qualified as a member, along with his father, for the Million Dollar Round Table, the industry's method of recognizing extraordinary agents. Today, Bruce carries on the tradition his father began, and he recently received the signal honor of being elected president of the prestigious National Association of Life Underwriters, with its 125,000 underwriter members. His father still manages to qualify for the company's top club each year and helps keep the Holdrege sales of insurance in the forefront.

Career agents today quite obviously no longer share Bill Jaeger's original antipathy toward group insurance. While most of them would probably agree with their senior vice-president for individual insurance, John Elken, that "social insurance does intrude upon private insurance," they would at the same time give a hearty amen to his additional statement that "while group insurance may now serve needs which once were met by individual insurance, it has been a natural development and a strong stimulant in the individual insurance marketplace." Most of the sales force have learned well Merv Cramer's sales techniques of tying individual life sales to prominent group clients. "Here is a list of some of the nation's top businesses which have selected Bankers Life to handle the pension plans for their employees, involving hundreds of thousands of dollars in premiums," Cramer would casually drop in conversation to a wide-eyed prospective Los Angeles client. "Now about this plan that you are considering ..." It is still an effective line.

Just how effective it could be is best illustrated by Norb Koch of the Richard A. Larson, CLU, St. Paul agency, who in 1978 was to be designated Agent of the Year. In that year, on the eve of Bankers Life's centennial, Koch was to set an all-time record by selling over $11 million of insurance, to bring his lifetime total to well over $125 million. Koch estimates that 70 percent of his production comes from what he calls "sponsored sales," that is, insurance bought by a client for someone else, primarily employers for their employees.

In achieving his remarkable record, Koch has persistently stressed to prospective clients the kind of flexibility—what he calls "the self-completion features"—that life insurance provides and that gives insurance an edge over any other form of saving. Koch, not content to rest upon past achievement, always keeps a sharp eye on potential sales fields that are relatively untapped. He notes with interest the increasingly larger portion of the national income that women are receiving, and women as wage earners have not been an important market for insurance. To develop this market fully, however, Koch believes that the insurance industry needs more women agents, and "when I say the business needs more female agents, I don't mean twice as many, but rather a hundred times more." Koch's oldest son, Dick, is now selling for Bankers Life, and perhaps Koch is already anticipating the day when one of his young daughters may be part of the Bankers Life family—perhaps even Agent of the Year by tapping that new and growing market.

As indicated earlier, group insurance and pensions have, of necessity, developed a somewhat different sales force. Because of the variety of programs possible and the far more intricate details that had to be mastered, group sales developed a force of one hundred experts, who are salaried, receiving no commissions but earning bonuses based on results. Their task includes not only selling the client but also selling the broker and the agent on the merits of Bankers Life group products. These group and pension managers not only must be highly trained in the intricacies of a rapidly changing and expanding field of insurance but also must be highly skilled in interpersonal relations. Bill Schneider and his vice-president for sales, Bob Larson, have been able to build such a force that could work effectively with Bankers Life's own agents and with major brokerage agencies in the large metropolitan areas of the nation. Special and distinctly different attention must be given to both Holdrege, Nebraska, and New York, New York.

From that early moment when the directors of the Association decided to make its certificates of membership available to others than a select group of bank employees, Bankers Life has always been interested in growth. Particularly from the time that George Kuhns first entered the home office, the company has vigorously pushed expansion with an aggressive sales policy and a constant attention for the development of new products and better service which would capture the attention of the market. But like a young boy who eats voraciously and vigorously pursues a body-building regimen only to discover to his own amazement that last month's clothes no longer fit him, so Bankers Life, somewhat to its own surprise, suddenly realized in the early 1960s that it had become one of the giants in the industry. It had become something more than just a large midwestern insurance company. It now ranked among the twenty largest life insurance companies in the nation.

With that realization there came a serious concern for the company's public corporate image. Bankers Life, to be sure, had long been piqued by the fact that it had never received the recognition it deserved even within its own city and state. Most Iowans continued to think of their oldest insurance company, Equitable of Iowa, as being the state's largest insurance company, even though Bankers Life had since the early 1920s far exceeded its friendly rival in the Gothic skyscraper down the street in the amount of life insurance it had in force.

Even more irritating to Bankers Life were the fifty or more national insurance companies who had incorporated the word "Bankers" or "Bankers Life" in their company names. The public, not surprisingly, often confused Bankers Life with these similarly named organizations. Bankers Life had some justification in believing that a few of these companies were deliberately cashing in on its own reputation for integrity, sound fiscal management, and prompt payment of claims to fool the public. It was not considered advisable, however, to bring suits against these unwanted namesakes, for quite likely "Bankers Life" would be considered by the courts to be a generic term, and as the name had not been registered as a trademark, its exclusive use could not be protected by any one company. Imitation was a form of unwelcome flattery for which apparently the only remedial response was to make the oldest and strongest Bankers Life Company so well known that there could be no confusion in the public mind.

In 1965 President Bucknell asked John M. K. Abbott, the recently retired vice-president for public relations of New York Life Insurance Company, to serve as a consultant to advise the company on how it might improve its public relations operations. Bankers Life had never had a public relations department as such. The company secretary, Bert Mills, in the period from the 1920s until his retirement in the mid-1940s, had been the nearest approach to a public relations officer that the company had had. After his departure, the major functions of public relations had been shared by sales promotion and the advertising departments, with Edward Leader, as advertising manager, taking the major responsibility.

Abbott in his report to Bucknell, dated February 1, 1966, was properly critical of how a company of its size and importance was handling its public relations. He recommended that Bankers Life create a separate public relations department which could, in addition to other duties, "function as a service department, making sound public relations counsel and assistance available to other departments throughout the Company."

President Bucknell was quick to seize upon Abbott's recommendations and to implement them. In Walter Walsh, then employed by Oscar Mayer Co., Bucknell found the kind of public relations director Abbott had called for. In 1967 Walsh organized the new department and reorganized the company's publications. To replace the *Our Home Office* magazine, a new journal, *Comment*, much more readable in style and format, was created. It was an appropriate supplement to *Onward* magazine, largely directed toward the sales agents in the field.

Early in the 1960s, the company employed the famous scientific pollster Gallup and Associates to conduct a national survey of Bankers Life's public image. The results confirmed what the company already knew. Bankers Life, paradoxically, was too little known considering its size and importance within the insurance field to the general public and at the same time it was too well known within the insurance industry for its integrity and strength and hence the many similarly named companies. With the results of this poll in hand, the officers decided to take decisive action. The national advertising budget, which had been only $80,000 in 1947, was increased to an annual sum of $325,000 by 1968. Bankers Life in 1968, along with such companies as General Electric, Holiday Inns of America, Bell & Howell, and the Campbell Soup Co., became one of the sponsors of the NBC *Today* show, and Hugh Downs brought the message of Bankers Life insurance to a nationwide television audience. A Chicago design firm of Chapman, Goldsmith and Yamasaki was employed to give the company a unique and instantly recognizable abstract logo mark, a black and a white interlocking link imposed upon a green background. The company in its advertising also added the significant article *the* to its name. Henceforth it was *THE BANKERS LIFE*. The implication was clear. There might be scores of imitations but only one true Bankers Life Company.

Beginning in 1968 Walsh also developed a public relations program that sought to meet the demands of a growing consumerism movement. Instead of using advertising only to offer traditional life insurance sales pitches for particular policies, Walsh developed a program that empathized with the consumer's problem of making intelligent choices from the vast array of policies being sold by the eighteen hundred life insurance companies in the United States. The messages, advertised both on network television and in major mass-circulation magazines, offered the public a variety of objective booklets on insurance illustrating how individuals could make rational decisions in respect to their life insurance purchases. Three of these booklets were:

"Insurance Handbook: 50 answers to basic questions on life and health insurance."

"How to Select the Right Life Insurance Company."

"How Much Life Insurance Do I Need? How Much Life Insurance Can I Afford?"

Bankers Life was thus a pioneer within the industry in asking the public to think of themselves as "consumers of insurance." That these booklets filled an obvious public need and helped to counteract the growing consumer and governmental criticism is evident by the fact that since 1968, hundreds of thousands of copies have been requested by the general public.

Much credit must be given to Bucknell for the emphasis he gave to Bankers Life's external relations. But of equal importance to the company's success has been its internal relations. As Bankers Life has grown in size and complexity, its internal organization has, of necessity, reflected these changes. Even Nollen, who did not retire from the Board of Directors until 1957, would have had difficulty finding his way through the organizational chart of the company by the late 1970s. The creation of organizational structures that could serve an ever-expanding, ever more demanding business, and the designation of the right people to inhabit those structures have been the outstanding managerial achievements of Presidents Bucknell, Allen, and Houser. But at the same time that this more complex structure was being created, quite remarkably Bankers Life has been able to maintain a sense of community. This has proved invaluable not only for office morale but also in terms of actual program development. In a company of Bankers Life's size there is remarkably easy and direct communications between departments and divisions. In the executive dining room or in the buffet dining hall, actuaries can learn from their informal discussions with the lawyers what legal problems resulting from the latest governmental regulations must be taken into consideration for future planning, and the sales executives know in advance the progress that is being made in developing new products.

This intramural understanding over the long years of the company's history has made it possible for the top executives to have a rather complete knowledge of all the operations of the company. Although some of the officials wish that lateral mobility were as possible in the company as upward mobility is, some of the company's key figures have known a considerable degree of lateral as well as upward movement. For example, Ray Cassell, who retired in 1977 as senior vice-president and secretary of the company, was able to serve in those offices with the high distinction that he did because in the forty-one years he was with the company he had acquired firsthand knowledge of most of its operations. Beginning in the policy loan department, writing "due from" letters, he was later moved to planning. After serving as a staff officer with Patton's army in World War II, he returned to Bankers Life and was soon engaged in writing job descriptions for every department in the company. After being recalled for military duty in Korea, he again returned to Bankers Life to work on new data-processing systems, thus preparing the way for conversion to the computer. By the time he became secretary of the company in 1956, his lateral movements had carried him into almost every cranny and compartment of the home office. He was certainly fully qualified to serve as senior vice-president of corporate services, in the broadest possible meaning of that term. And for his services to the community of Des Moines, which included development of the Community Improvement, Inc., for summer employment of the disadvantaged, Cassell in 1978 was honored by the Des Moines Area Conference of Christians and Jews.

Former President Bucknell, in commenting upon the last twenty-five years of the company's history, said that in his opinion one major "thread which should run through that history would deal with this all-important problem of management. A company will only be as good as its people." Or to put it another way, the departmental and divisional squares on an organizational chart may be neat and logical, the computer may hum away quietly and efficiently, but happily neither the chart nor the machine is self-sustaining. The human element is still indispensable. Insurance may be a business built upon mathematical probabilities and mass statistics, but its concern must continue to be directed toward the individual person, both as employee and customer. It is that mutuality of interest, as Houser has said, that makes "the word 'mutual' in the company's corporate nomenclature meaningful."

For Bankers Life that mutuality of interest has paid handsome dividends—not only in achieving the fastest growth rate of any major company over the last five years within the industry and not only in providing the market with new and better products and in satisfying its customers with prompt service and understanding concern, but also in having the satisfaction of knowing that growth and integrity, bigness and compassion, can be complementary, not antagonistic, terms. There is a very large dividend, indeed, in knowing that one's company has won for itself not only the envy but also the admiration of its competitors.

The history of this company began with Edward Temple, a forty-eight-year-old banker from Chariton, Iowa, arriving in Des Moines in the spring of 1879 to call upon the Casady family in order to explain to them a simple but novel idea he had for a life insurance association for bankers. Temple was well received by the Casadys, a prosperous, pioneer family in this rough, unfinished capital town. So Temple stayed and built his Association and lived for thirty more years, lived to see his beloved Association prosper and grow into a business with assets of over $13 million and nearly $500 million worth of insurance in force.

This particular chapter of what must be regarded as the unfinished account of Mr. Temple's child comes to a conclusion one hundred years later. Should Temple return to Des Moines to commemorate this significant milestone in his company's history, he would find himself an alien in an alien land. If he were to ask his way, as he surely would, to the Bankers Life office, he would be directed up High Street to the crest of Piety Hill, where in his day the Weitz homestead and the old Presbyterian Church had stood. With growing disbelief, he would climb the rainbow granite steps and enter into this monumental home office that housed his company. What had all of this cost? With trembling fear, he would introduce himself and ask to see the latest annual report—for the year 1978. Incredible—surely, there were far too many figures in each line here:

Insurance in force, $27 billion
Assets, $5.8 billion
Premium income, $1.3 billion
Benefits paid, $701 million

What was Bankers Life selling these days? Certainly something more than $2,000 certificates of membership in his Association. Group insurance, pensions, property liability? What do these terms mean? And then the man who sat in the president's chair would proudly display pamphlets describing two of Bankers Life's most recent products: a new group health insurance plan, PAT 500, which encourages, through its benefits schedule, out-of-hospital preventative care and treatment, and most remarkable of all, a new individual life policy, called adjustable life, which allows the policyholder periodically to change both his premium costs and his coverage—a revolutionary new concept in individual life insurance.

When asked if he would like to see the electronic computers, Temple would probably at that point turn and flee. One hundred years couldn't produce that many changes surely. It was beyond even immortal comprehension.

The century of Bankers Life's existence covers the most revolutionary technological period in human history. Edward Temple would feel far more at home going back one hundred years to 1779 than he would going forward to the present moment. Yet some things

have remained as constants in this turbulent century. Certain principles and ideals have persisted. Had the ghost of Edward Temple stayed
long enough to rummage around a bit in the company archives, he
might have found some comforting evidence of constancy. He might,
for example, have found the letter his eighth successor to the
presidency, Robert Houser, wrote in 1975 in response to a note from a
former director, Gardner Cowles, congratulating Houser upon his
reelection to the presidency. "We do have a good Company," Houser
agreed with Cowles. "I've seen it from many angles over the many
years since 1936. Somehow we've managed over the years to combine
a high level of integrity with an innovative approach to doing
business. We'll work to keep it that way." And so they have—for the
past one hundred years. Edward Temple would have had no difficulty
understanding that letter. He might well have written it himself.

Appendix

GROWTH RATES OF THE BANKERS LIFE AND THE LIFE INSURANCE INDUSTRY: 1950 – 1978

Using three widely accepted measurements of size—premium income, assets, and life insurance in force—the following three graphs compare the rate of growth of The Bankers Life to the industry averages of over 1,700 United States life insurance companies. The measures are shown as a percentage of the base year 1950, using a base figure 100.

ASSETS

Assets consist of the funds invested and managed by a life insurance company for future payments to policyowners and beneficiaries. The graph shows the growth rate for The Bankers Life steadily climbing above the rate for the industry from 1950–1970, and then accelerating that difference during the 1970s.

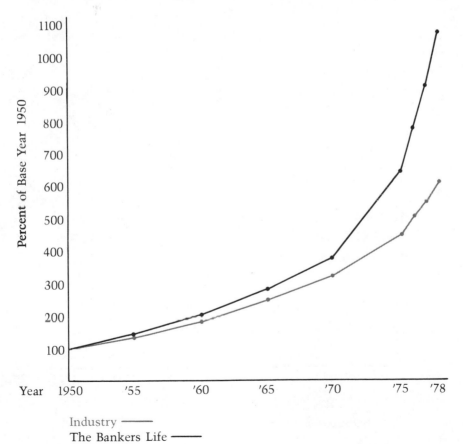

PREMIUM INCOME

Premium income reflects the sales success in all types of business written by life insurance companies. It is the total amount paid to a company during the year by policyowners for all life, health, and pension plans. The graph shows The Bankers Life consistently above the industry average in premium growth, with that difference dramatically increasing during the 1970s.

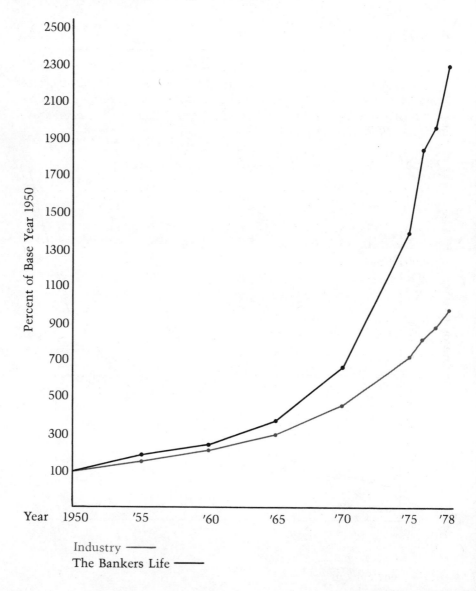

Year

Industry ——
The Bankers Life ——

LIFE INSURANCE IN FORCE

This measure consists of the total life insurance protection, both individual and group, provided by life insurance companies. As the graph shows, the growth rate of The Bankers Life has been increasing steadily above that of the industry average during the last decade.

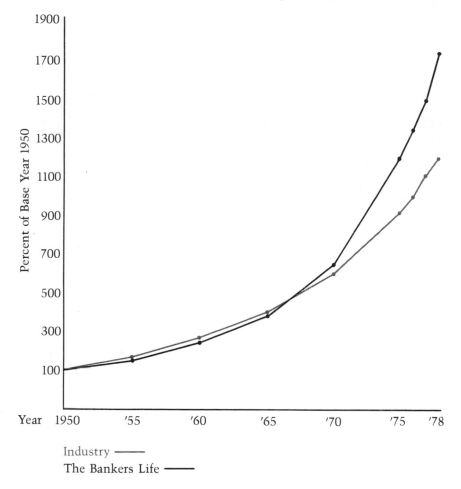

Industry ———
The Bankers Life ———

MARKET SHARE

Using these three measurements of size, it is possible to illustrate The Bankers Life's share of the total U.S. life insurance market. Shown as a percentage of the industry's totals, The Bankers Life's market share of premiums, assets, and life insurance in force has increased significantly in recent years.

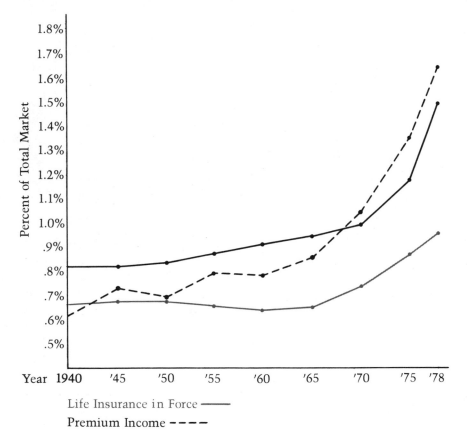

Life Insurance in Force ———
Premium Income ― ― ― ―
Assets ———

NET INTEREST RATE BEFORE FEDERAL INCOME TAX

The investment policy of The Bankers Life reflects the company's goals to secure the highest rate of return on assets commensurate with safety. A philosophy of diversifying investments in response to changing economic conditions has contributed to The Bankers Life achieving rates of return above the industry average after 1950.

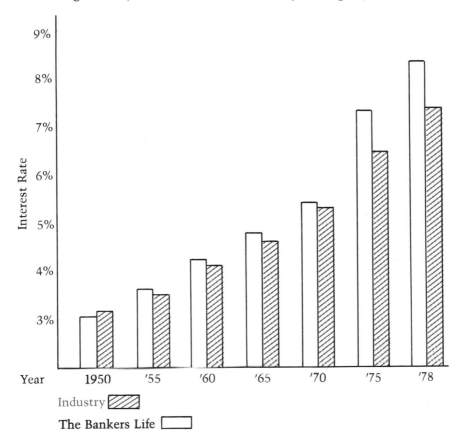

Industry

The Bankers Life

HISTORICAL SUMMARY OF LIFE INSURANCE MEASURES OF THE BANKERS LIFE *(Millions)*

Year	Assets	Insurance in Force	Premium Income
1879	$ .001	$ .1	Not Available
1880	.008	.4	Not Available
1890	.7	29.3	.2
1900	4.2	143.3	1.1
1910	15.4	451.1	4.4
1920	44.5	555.5	13.3
1930	148.9	941.9	32.7
1940	251.5	762.9	24.0
1950	534.1	1,559.6	57.1
1955	791.4	2,468.8	100.0
1960	1,093.5	3,760.2	135.4
1965	1,505.7	5,907.2	214.4
1970	2,048.7	10,282.6	384.2
1975	3,419.7	18,659.6	796.3
1978	5,771.0	27,163.4	1,308.4

SUMMARY OF LIFE INSURANCE MEASURES OF THE BANKERS LIFE, 1950 – 1979

LIFE INSURANCE IN FORCE *(Millions)*

	Individual	Group	Total	Yearly Increase	Percent Increase
1950	$ 1,255	$ 305	$ 1,560	$ 117	8.1%
1955	1,566	902	2,468	242	10.9
1960	2,078	1,682	3,760	211	5.9
1965	3,034	2,873	5,907	684	13.1
1970	4,948	5,335	10,283	889	9.5
1975	8,301	10,359	18,660	1,933	11.6
1978	11,832	15,331	27,163	3,798	16.3

TIME REQUIRED TO ACHIEVE VARIOUS LIFE INSURANCE TOTALS

Total Life Insurance in Force	Year Attained	Time Required
$ 1 billion	1945	56 yrs.
2 billion	1954	9 yrs.
4 billion	1962	7½ yrs.
6 billion	1966	4 yrs.
8 billion	1968	2½ yrs.
10 billion	1970	2 yrs.
12 billion	1972	2 yrs.
14 billion	1973	15 mos.
16 billion	1974	10 mos.
18 billion	1975	13 mos.
20 billion	1976	11 mos.
22 billion	1977	11 mos.
24 billion	1978	7 mos.
26 billion	1978	7 mos.

PREMIUM INCOME *(Millions)*

	Individual				Group		
	Life & Annuity	Health	Total		Life & Health	Pension	Total
1950	$ 38.4	$ 0	$ 38.4		$ 6.0	$ 12.7	$ 18.7
1955	45.1	.3	45.4		18.1	36.5	54.6
1960	52.2	.9	53.1		42.7	39.6	82.3
1965	69.3	2.4	71.7		73.2	69.5	142.7
1970	102.7	6.0	108.7		163.9	111.6	275.5
1975	169.7	14.2	183.9		300.2	312.2	612.4
1978	237.3	16.5	253.8		400.7	653.9	1,054.6

	Company Total	Yearly Increase	Percent Increase
1950	$ 57.1	$ 5.0	9.6%
1955	100.0	15.9	18.9
1960	135.4	11.1	8.9
1965	214.4	18.6	9.5
1970	384.2	60.9	18.8
1975	796.3	169.6	27.1
1978	1,308.4	186.0	16.6

HALL OF FAME MEMBERS

These 58 agents of The Bankers Life have been enshrined in the "Hall of Fame" by having qualified for 20 or more "Top Clubs." The list shows the year each entered, the total number of Top Club qualifications through 1978 and the agency.

1949 E. G. (Grady) Bryant (25)
      Spokane Agency
1949 J. (Joseph) Janciar (29)
      Pittsburgh Agency
1957 P. O. (Paul) Day (39)
      Toledo Agency
1958 A. M. (Alan) Cannon (39)
      Boise Agency
1958 W. H. Deppey (20)
      Cedar Rapids Agency
1960 C. R. (Carl) Hendrickson (37)
      Lincoln Agency
1962 A. M. Glick (23)
      Ottumwa Agency
1962 C. H. (Cec) Luxford (23)
      Omaha Agency
1962 E. F. (Ewin) Maxwell (30)
      Detroit Agency
1963 R. (Ruth) Day (28)
      Detroit Agency
1964 L. (Whit) Whitsitt (22)
      Decatur Agency
1965 W. S. (Walt) Evans (30)
      Houston Agency
1965 V. A. (Babe) LeVoir, CLU (32)
      Minneapolis Agency
1966 D. G. (Dean) Ball (20)
      Madison Agency
1966 S. C. (Sandy) Brinsmaid (31)
      Buffalo-Dillon Agency
1966 E. G. (Gene) Flick, CLU (31)
      Minneapolis Agency
1966 H. E. (Harry) Gidel, CLU (25)
      Decatur Agency
1966 W. L. (Bill) Leavy, CLU (26)
      Fort Worth Agency
1966 S. S. (Sam) Loyer, CLU (25)
      Columbus Agency

1966 A. H. (Art) Neuhaus (24)
      Milwaukee Agency
1966 J. M. (John) Sisk, Sr. (29)
      Milwaukee Agency
1966 F. (Floyd) Smith (28)
      El Paso Agency
1966 H. (Harold) Van Every, CLU (31)
      Minneapolis Agency
1968 W. A. Doherty (20)
      Portland Agency
1968 S. D. (Sam) Flanz (30)
      Houston Agency
1968 B. A. (Bud) Howard (28)
      Boise Agency
1968 C. L. (Chuck) Seibert (26)
      Buffalo-Dillon Agency
1968 R. J. (Jim) Weaver (20)
      Milwaukee Agency
1969 E. W. (Erv) Koenig (24)
      Milwaukee Agency
1969 F. C. (Fred) Neiman (26)
      Pittsburgh Agency
1970 R. C. (Pete) Gilmore, CLU (27)
      Washington, D. C., Agency
1970 E. W. (Dutch) Shellenberger (22)
      Chicago-Thomson Agency
1971 G. E. (Glen) Berge (26)
      Salt Lake City Agency
1971 F. B. (Henry) Ford (27)
      El Paso Agency
1971 J. F. (Jay) Smith (21)
      Oklahoma City Agency
1971 H. M. (Harry) Vondrak (24)
      Lincoln Agency
1972 N. (Norb) Koch (26)
      St. Paul Agency
1972 G. O. (Gus) Larsen, CLU (26)
      Rockford Agency
1972 F. A. (Floyd) Raymond (26)
      Lincoln Agency

1972 H. R. (Rudge) Vifquain (26)
      Lincoln Agency
1973 C. (Cliff) Ellingson (25)
      Mason City Agency
1973 F. C. (Fritz) Zeh (25)
      Pittsburgh Agency
1974 M. A. (Milt) Link (24)
      Seattle Agency
1975 E. R. (Ernie) Brinkman (23)
      Lincoln Agency
1975 C. A. (Sid) Hiner (23)
      Lincoln Agency
1975 E. C. (Ellsworth) Hunter (20)
      Lincoln Agency
1975 J. M. (Johnny) Jones, Jr. (23)
      San Antonio Agency
1976 A. D. Holland, CLU (22)
      Dallas Agency
1977 C. J. (Cec) Bogard, CLU (21)
      St. Paul Agency

1977 B. C. (Bruce) Hendrickson,
      CLU (21) Lincoln Agency
1977 C. R. (Chuck) Peterson (21)
      Rockford Agency
1977 G. G. Robinson (21)
      Tulsa Agency
1978 W. (Wendell) Jensen (20)
      Lincoln Agency
1978 P. J. (Phil) McElroy (20)
      Minneapolis Agency
1978 P. F. (Fred) Naylor (20)
      Portland Agency
1978 J. S. M. (Jim) Sandison,
      CLU (20) Encino Agency
1979 R. W. (Dick) Beggs (20)
      Madison Agency
1979 R. E. (Bob) Krieger (20)
      Minneapolis Agency

MASTER AGENCY BUILDERS TROPHY CONTEST

Traditionally referred to as "The Angel," this trophy is awarded to a qualifying agency manager who does the best over-all job of sound agency building. The Agency Builders Trophy remains in the winner's possession for one year. Winning The Angel is a sign of both quality management and top production.

MANAGER, AGENCY

1961 W. A. Fraser, CLU, Lincoln
1962 O. H. Gudmunson, Los
      Angeles
1963 R. E. Olson, Des Moines
1964 O. H. Gudmunson, Los
      Angeles
1965 E. J. Collins, Philadelphia
1966 J. L. Thorngren, CLU, San
      Antonio
1967 J. L. Thorngren, CLU, San
      Antonio
1968 J. L. Thorngren, CLU, San
      Antonio
1969 E. J. Collins, Philadelphia

1970 D. T. Miller, Boise
1971 D. T. Miller, Boise
1972 D. T. Miller, Boise
1973 D. T. Miller, Boise
1974 Irwin Katzman, CLU,
      Buffalo-Katzman
1975 Morry Reisman, CLU,
      Lincolnwood
1976 Richard E. Olson, Des
      Moines
1977 Richard E. Olson, Des
      Moines
1978 Morry Reisman, CLU,
      Lincolnwood

BROKERAGE BUILDERS TROPHY CONTEST

This trophy, first awarded in 1969, is presented to the qualifying brokerage agency manager who accomplishes the most productive job of brokerage development during the year. MART qualification is a prerequisite for winning the brokerage builders trophy.

MANAGER, AGENCY

1969 Gerson M. Sparer, CLU, New York City
1970 Elliot G. Lengel, CLU, Newark
1971 Elliot G. Lengel, CLU, Newark
1972 Dwight R. Otto, CLU, Dallas
1973 Gerson M. Sparer, CLU, New York City

1974 Alf O. Olsen, CLU, Philadelphia
1975 Gerson M. Sparer, CLU, New York City
1976 John J. Waddick, Chicago
1977 Melvin A. Pachter, Los Angeles
1978 John N. Neighbors, CLU, Houston

SPECIAL BROKERAGE AGENCY TROPHY CONTEST

Begun in 1978, this competition is designed to recognize the managing director who does the best job of developing his special brokerage agency. Qualification is based on production and first year amounts.

MANAGER, AGENCY

1978 Asher Schapiro, New York

LEADING INDIVIDUAL AGENCIES

DATE	AGENCY	MANAGER	PRODUCTION
			Ordinary Only
1920	Dallas	William Bacon	$ 5,307,007
1921	San Antonio	Cherry & Cherry	6,013,024
1922	Indianapolis	Elbert Storer	6,142,600
1923	Chicago	DeForest Bowman	6,441,702
1924	Indianapolis	Elbert Storer	6,206,122
1925	Chicago	DeForest Bowman	6,887,219
1926	Indianapolis	Elbert Storer	7,606,191
1927	Chicago	DeForest Bowman	7,778,171
1928	Chicago	DeForest Bowman	6,104,720
1929	Indianapolis	Elbert Storer	5,737,708
1930	Indianapolis	Elbert Storer	4,863,122
1931	Indianapolis	Elbert Storer	3,552,300
1932	Chicago	DeForest Bowman	3,111,350
1933	Chicago	DeForest Bowman	2,373,664
1934	Des Moines	J. A. Spargur	2,535,557
1935	Indianapolis	H. E. Storer	2,942,270
1936	Des Moines	W. K. Niemann	2,368,421
1937	Des Moines	W. K. Niemann	2,773,566
1938	Des Moines	W. K. Niemann	3,004,705
1939	Des Moines	W. K. Niemann	2,751,174
1940	Des Moines	W. K. Niemann	3,208,185
1941	Des Moines	W. K. Niemann	3,597,653
1942	Des Moines	W. K. Niemann	3,874,941
1943	Des Moines	W. K. Niemann	3,904,499
1944	Des Moines	W. K. Niemann	5,351,852
1945	Des Moines	W. K. Niemann	4,627,526
1946	Des Moines	W. K. Niemann	6,313,316
1947	Lincoln	W. A. Fraser	6,982,525
1948	Des Moines	W. K. Niemann	5,555,960

1949	Minneapolis	R. E. Shay	$ 4,884,917
1950	Minneapolis	R. E. Shay	6,137,775
1951	Minneapolis	R. E. Shay	6,289,426
1952	Minneapolis	R. E. Shay	6,276,222
			Combined Ordinary & Health
1953	Lincoln	W. A. Fraser	6,849,275
1954	Lincoln	W. A. Fraser	8,835,362
1955	Lincoln	W. A. Fraser	8,252,736
1956	Minneapolis	R. J. Bjorklund	7,781,744
1957	Lincoln	W. A. Fraser	11,082,588
1958	Lincoln	W. A. Fraser	11,169,936
1959	Lincoln	W. A. Fraser	14,235,057
1960	Lincoln	W. A. Fraser	14,846,324
1961	Lincoln	W. A. Fraser	15,673,384
1962	Lincoln	Perry O. Moore	16,075,688
			Combined Ordinary, Health & Group
1963	Lincoln	Perry O. Moore	18,760,168
1964	Des Moines	Richard E. Olson	21,685,205
1965	Des Moines	Richard E. Olson	24,260,979
1966	Des Moines	Richard E. Olson	25,096,549
1967	Des Moines	Richard E. Olson	32,308,146
1968	Des Moines	Richard E. Olson	35,501,448
1969	Des Moines	Richard E. Olson	43,129,182
1970	Des Moines	Richard E. Olson	41,857,515
1971	Des Moines	Richard E. Olson	40,249,731
1972	Des Moines	Richard E. Olson	47,313,076
1973	Tampa	Angus Williams, Jr.	52,690,597
1974	Des Moines	Richard E. Olson	58,832,618
1975	Des Moines	Richard E. Olson	65,077,650
1976	Des Moines	Richard E. Olson	81,912,166
1977	Des Moines	Richard E. Olson	94,874,023
1978	Des Moines	Richard E. Olson	101,290,505

AGENT SALES LEADERS

The Bankers Life became a mutual legal reserve company in 1911. Since that time annual agent sales leaders have been recognized in various ways:

1915–1926	"Company Production Leader"
1927–1945/46	"President of President's Premier Club"
1946/47–1969	"President of President's Club"
1970–1972	"Man of the Year"
1973–present	"Agent of the Year"

1915 G. F. Murrell, Pittsburgh
1916 G. F. Murrell, Pittsburgh
1917 A. T. Kirk
1918 G. F. Murrell, Pittsburgh
1919 G. F. Murrell, Pittsburgh
1920 G. F. Murrell, Pittsburgh
1921 H. C. Walburn, W. Virginia
1922 H. C. Walburn, W. Virginia
1923 W. A. Hinshaw, Iowa
1924 W. A. Hinshaw, Iowa
1925 J. H. Pope, Cedar Rapids
1926 W. B. Mahaffa, Des Moines
1927 Joseph Hunciar, Pittsburgh
1928 Joseph Hunciar, Pittsburgh
1929 W. B. Mahaffa, Des Moines
1930 W. B. Mahaffa, Des Moines
1931 J. H. Rowe, Chicago
1932 J. H. Rowe, Chicago
1933 H. M. Teare, New York City
1934 J. H. Rowe, Chicago
1935 J. H. Rowe, Chicago
1936 J. H. Rowe, Chicago
1937 T. S. Reinhard, New York City
1938 G. A. Specht, Minneapolis
1939 H. M. Teare, New York City
1940-41 Joseph Janciar, Pittsburgh
1941-42 W. B. Mahaffa, Des Moines
1942-43 C. S. Huffman, Decatur
1943-44 C. S. Huffman, Decatur
1944-45 C. R. Hendrickson, Lincoln
1945-46 R. D. Wright, Cleveland

1946-47 John M. Sisk, Milwaukee
1947-48 John M. Sisk, Milwaukee
1948-49 John M. Sisk, Milwaukee
1950 John M. Sisk, Milwaukee
1951 John M. Sisk, Milwaukee
1952 John M. Sisk, Milwaukee
1953 Robert D. Wright, Cleveland
1954-55 Robert D. Wright, Cleveland
1955-56 Robert D. Wright, Cleveland
1956-57 Robert D. Wright, Cleveland
1957-58 David R. Meredith, Des Moines
1958-59 Robert J. Gallivan, Jr., St. Paul
1960 Norb Koch, Minneapolis
1961 Norb Koch, Minneapolis
1962 Norb Koch, Minneapolis
1963 Robert D. Wright, Cleveland
1964 Norb Koch, Minneapolis
1965 Robert J. Gallivan, Jr., St. Paul
1966 Robert J. Gallivan, Jr. St. Paul
1967 Robert J. Gallivan, Jr. St. Paul
1968 Robert J. Gallivan, Jr. St. Paul
1969 Robert J. Gallivan, Jr. St. Paul
1970 Norb Koch, Minneapolis
1971 Norb Koch, Minneapolis

1972 Norb Koch, Minneapolis
1973 Frank M. Lorenzo, Sr.,
      Tampa
1974 Frank M. Lorenzo, Sr.,
      Tampa
1975 Frank M. Lorenzo, Sr.,
      Tampa

1976 Roy L. D'Alessandro,
      Pittsburgh
1977 Richard W. Beggs, CLU,
      Madison
1978 Nicholas J. Lamoriello,
      Providence
1979 Norb Koch, St. Paul

REGIONAL GROUP CONTESTS

Three regional group contests, held annually, recognize the leading producing group offices of The Bankers Life. They include:
Performance Pacer Contest, based on total production credits.
Case Derby Contest, based on new case count.
Premium Sweepstakes, based on contest premium weighted for type of business.
In addition the Individual Pacer Contest recognizes individual production based on total production credits.

PREMIUM SWEEPSTAKES CONTEST

	TERRITORY, REGIONAL GROUP MANAGER		TERRITORY, REGIONAL GROUP MANAGER
1944	Chicago, Tom Moore	1962	Des Moines, Charles DeWinter
1945	Chicago, Tom Moore	1963	Chicago, Frank Weisman
1946	Buffalo, George Lewis	1964	Chicago, Frank Weisman
1947	Chicago, Tom Moore	1965	Detroit, Wes Bray
1948	Houston-Dallas, Ross Fox	1966	St. Louis, Bob Schreiber
1949	Portland, Phil Berthiaume	1967	Des Moines, Bob Schroeder
1950	San Francisco, Gene Severin	1968	Milwaukee, Dave Barton
1951	Los Angeles, Tom Rainey	1969	New York, Wes Bray
1952	Houston, Ross Fox	1970	Minneapolis, Rich Rostvold
1953	Milwaukee, Tom Moore	1971	Chicago, Frank Weisman
1954	New York, Gren Vale	1972	New York, Wes Bray
1955	New York, Gren Vale	1973	Des Moines, Bob Schroeder
1956	Des Moines, Charles DeWinter	1974	Minneapolis, Dixon Jordan
1957	Des Moines, Charles DeWinter	1975	Seattle, Ed Lynde
1958	Milwaukee, Tom Moore	1976	Des Moines, Bob Schroeder
1959	Detroit, Frank Casey	1977	Milwaukee, Wally Dinsmoor
1960	Chicago, Frank Weisman	1978	New York, Mike Saunders
1961	Des Moines, Charles DeWinter		

PERFORMANCE PACER CONTEST *(Total Production Credits)*

TERRITORY, REGIONAL GROUP MANAGER

1969 Oklahoma City, Scott Coffman
1970 Minneapolis, Rich Rostvold
1971 Boston, Bill Burke
1972 New York, Wes Bray
1973 Des Moines, Bob Schroeder
1974 Omaha, Ken Fridrich
1975 Des Moines, Bob Schroeder
1976 Des Moines, Bob Schroeder
1977 Detroit-Cleveland, Bill Thayer
1978 Cleveland, Gene Mills

CASE DERBY CONTEST *(new contest case count)*

TERRITORY, REGIONAL GROUP MANAGER

1944 Portland, Phil Berthiaume
1945 Pittsburgh, Edward Optekar
1946 Los Angeles, Tom Rainey
1947 Portland, Phil Berthiaume
1948 Des Moines, Charles DeWinter
1949 Portland, Phil Berthiaume
1950 Buffalo, George Lewis
1951 Portland, Phil Berthiaume
1952 Los Angeles, Tom Rainey
1953 Houston, Ross Fox
1954 Chicago, Frank Weisman
1955 Chicago, Frank Weisman
1956 Chicago, Frank Weisman
1957 Atlanta, Frank Smith
1958 Houston, Steve Whatley
1959 Los Angeles, Tom Rainey
1960 Phoenix, Stan Brotherton
1961 Des Moines, Charles DeWinter

1962 Atlanta, Frank Smith
1963 Philadelphia, Joe Nally
1964 Philadelphia, Joe Nally
1965 Des Moines, Bob Schroeder
1966 Dallas, Ted Hahn
1967 Philadelphia, Joe Nally
1968 Phoenix, Stan Brotherton
1969 New York, Wes Bray
1970 Memphis, Will Stafford
1971 Memphis, Will Stafford
1972 Tie: Tampa, Dan Benshoof
      Memphis, Will Stafford
1973 Miami, Joe Steen
1974 Miami, Joe Steen
1975 Omaha, Ken Fridrich
1976 Pittsburgh, Dave Mosey
1977 Boston, Bill Burke
1978 Houston, Rich Rostvold

INDIVIDUAL PACER CONTEST
(Total Production Credits, Categories Are by Job Classification)

	ALL MANAGERS *(Except Regional)*	*ALL CONSULTANTS*
1975	Gene Mills, Cleveland	Mark Pedersen, Chicago
1976	Chad Sims, Des Moines	Dennis Peine, Miami
1977	Dick Fedro, Davenport	Bill Alexander, Cleveland
1978	Chad Sims, Des Moines	Bill Alexander, Cleveland

ALL OTHER REPRESENTATIVES INCLUDING GROUP OFFICE SUPERVISOR & GROUP ACCOUNT SUPERVISOR

1975	Herm Stahl, Tampa
1976	Bill Alexander, Cleveland
1977	Jan Jobe, Pittsburgh
1978	Jan Jobe, Pittsburgh

Index

About the Author

Joseph F. Wall, a native of Des Moines, Iowa, is an historian in the truest sense of the word. In addition to *Policies and People,* he is the author of six other books. He was selected to be one of the Bicentennial historians in the Bicentennial States and the Nation Series in 1977, authoring the *Iowa Bicentennial History.* In addition, many of his articles have been printed in encyclopedias, biographical dictionaries, and historical magazines.

    A graduate of Grinnell College in Grinnell, Iowa, with a masters and Ph.D. from Harvard and Columbia universities, respectively, Wall later returned to Grinnell as Professor of History and then the Dean of the History Department and Parker Professor of History. Dr. Wall is currently Professor of History and Chairman of the History Department at the State University of New York at Albany.

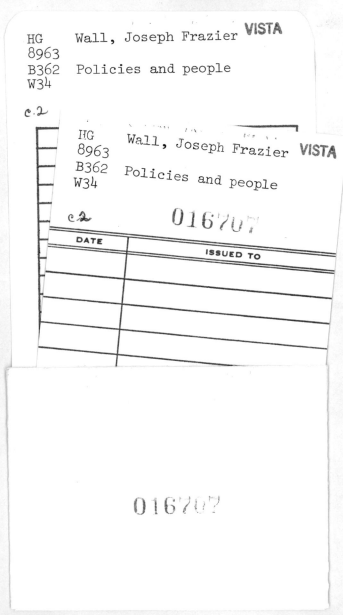